THE COVENANT OF LIFE

Table of Contents

AN ANTHOLOGY BY CHIEDZA NYANYIWA

THE COVENANT OF LIFE AND OTHER ESSAYS
Copyright © Chiedza Nyanyiwa, 2024
ISBN: 978-1-77933-856-3
Published by: Phoenix Publishing

ACKWOLEDGEMENTS

Firstly I would like to extend my most profound and deepest gratitude to God without whom this work would not exist and for whom it was written. Next I would like to thank my family for their belief in me. My friends, I thank you for being my biggest cheerleaders and of course my publisher for being excited for this work and for making this dream I have nurtured for years come to fruition.

DEDICATION

I dedicate this book to my grandparents Kudakwashe and Agathar Chamunorwa. It is your faith that has laid the foundation of my own.

CONTENTS

PART ONE

PART TWO: BEING

PART THREE: THE BUILDERS OF THE HOUSE

FOREWORD

In "The Covenant of Life and Other Essays," Chiedza Nyanyiwa presents a series of profound reflections on the profound intersections between faith, governance, and the trials of our times. Each essay is a thoughtful exploration of the enduring relevance and responsibility of the church in addressing the myriad challenges of a world beset by conflict and division.

At a time when the role of religious institutions in public policy and societal welfare is both celebrated and criticized, Nyanyiwa invites readers into a deep dialogue about the place of Christ and Christianity in contemporary society. Through eloquent prose and rigorous analysis, she examines the historical and theological foundations that define the church's position in the public sphere and its potential to influence policy making.

"The Covenant of Life and Other Essays" is not merely an academic discourse; it is a call to action. Nyanyiwa challenges believers and sceptics alike to reconsider the church's capability to foster peace and justice in an increasingly complex global landscape. She delves into scriptural and ethical discussions that remind us of God's initial intentions for humanity—peace, stewardship, and community.

As we navigate through these essays, we find ourselves confronted with the pressing question of how the church can remain true to its divine commission while effectively engaging with secular institutions and ideologies. The essays are imbued with a sense of urgency and hope, arguing for a renewed vision of Christian engagement that is both innovative and reflective of Christ's teachings.

This book is essential reading for anyone interested in the role of faith in shaping our world—be they scholars, church leaders, policymakers, or laypersons seeking deeper understanding of their faith's impact on public and personal realms. Chiedza Nyanyiwa's insights offer not only clarity but also a blueprint for how the covenant of life can be manifested in a world longing for redemption and direction.

Welcome to a compelling journey through the pages of "The Covenant of Life and Other Essays," where faith meets action, and where the church seeks to reclaim its transformative power in the world.

FAITH MUDIWA CHIPANGURA
(FOUNDER – PHOENIX PUBLISHING)

PART ONE

The first part of this anthology contains a collection of essays commenting on specific issues and books in the bible. The Covenant of Life explores God's journey with Israel and the foundations of his covenant. Exodus is an in-depth commentary on the book of Exodus followed by Leviticus, which does the same for the book of Leviticus. House of Dawn explores God's sovereignty through His promise to David and lastly on this section is Song Of A Barren Woman that looks at the role of women in the bible in God's story of grace and redemption. Tying these essays together is the theme of endeavouring to understand how God's journey with Israel was a foreshadowing of Christ. Essentially, the collective is an attempt to shine a light on Christ as the centrepiece of history upon which everything began, revolves around and is aiming towards.

THE COVENANT OF LIFE

Genesis 49 v 8-12
Judah, your brothers will praise you
You will grasp your enemies by the neck.
All your relatives will bow before you.
Judah my son is a young lion that has finished eating its prey.
Like a lion he crouches and lies down.
The sceptre will not depart from Judah,
nor the ruler's staff from his descendants
Until the coming of the One to whom it belongs,
the One whom all nations will honour.
He ties his foul to a grapevine.
the colt of his donkey to a choice vine.
He washes his clothes in wine,
his robes in blood of grapes.
His eyes are darker than wine,
and his teeth are whiter than milk

Look man has become like us, knowing both good and evil. What if he reaches out and eats from the tree of life," Genesis 3: 22. Eternity: this basically sums up the fate of existence. This reveals the single plight of the Light. What shall live and endure forever? The book of Genesis opens with God speaking earth into existence. Through the deep emptiness and darkness, He speaks light to be. From the surface of the deep waters, our God called the light to be. With this, begins His path of separating light from darkness. He separated the waters of the earth from the waters of the heavens and the space He called sky. From the dryness of the land He called life into being and He commanded each fruit to produce its seed and each seed to produce its like and its kind. He called the lights into being, stars, the sun and the moon, summoning them to mark the beginning of the ages and beyond them.

They would govern both night and day and they would guide humanity until the second coming. From the deep waters God summoned life to be and fish of all kind to swim there. To the sky, He called the birds and to the ground he summoned the animals. Within each, He put a seed which was meant to multiply these species. Finally from His image, He made human beings, male and female He made them in His likeness as the produce of His own seed, holiness. This was His command to them, "be fruitful and multiply. Fill the earth and govern it. Reign over the fish in the sea, the birds of the sky and the animals that scurry along the grounds." This was the command that sealed the fate of humanity forever.

Within the habitude of the humans, God had placed two trees symbolizing the eternal fate. The tree of eternal life from whose fruit eternity could be gained, the ability to live forever and be like God. From the second tree, was the fruit of the two potentials, good and evil which ultimately meant life and death. From these trees, man was forbidden to eat and because they were made in the image of God they obeyed. However the spirit prince of darkness worked up a plan and with a sweet and lying tongue he prompted man to disobey God. With this act, a seed was planted within man, a seed that gave birth to the struggle between good and evil upon the earth. The tale of humanity from there became one of the struggle between light and darkness but more importantly, it is a song sung by the Lord Himself and its enduring words are that He alone is life. Beyond good and bad is life and death. We saw in the account of creation that God spoke light into the world and set out to separate the light from the darkness and the things of heaven from those of this world. Here God had already laid out His plan in creation of separating the light and darkness and within humanity would always dwell the two potentials finding a home within the hearts of man. God walks with man through a voyage of discovery and teaches him the grand lesson that only light can give life. "Let the light separate from the darkness, call light day and darkness night: Let every seed bearing plant produce a plant of its kind." Yet man was forbidden to eat from the tree of light and darkness. A tree with two seeds produced two kinds of fruits light and darkness, Abel and Cain. Through the two brothers echoed the words of God when He said be fruitful and multiply. With Abel came the fruit that pleased the Lord for he had goodness within him but with Cain came a rotten fruit that did not please the Lord for he had darkness within him. The seed that had grown in Cain grew to despise the light that was in Abel and so Cain {darkness} murdered Abel {light}. With this the seed of good was extinguished and darkness ravaged the earth. With Abel fallen, the seed of darkness within Cain would grow forever to multiply until the Lord Himself could not put up with the sin of man and began the cleansing through Noah. So our Lord and God covered the earth with water once more, this time to purify the earth of darkness that had engulfed it. He cut short the lives of humans and sealed His promise that only goodness is eternal.

The Covenant of the Law

In His image He made them, male and female He made them yet when they sinned they surely died. Mankind is one with God because we are His creation but because of sin and the seed of darkness within man, we have shared the fate of Cain, heirs to his curse and cut off from the presence of God. We were cut off from the source of life and cut off from life itself. There is a war within humanity, a struggle between conscience and desire, between knowledge and will power.

Israel is the chosen servant of God to carry out His will, the flicker of hope and light. Israel was to be the seed placed within humanity and in her, light would be born. This light would carry not the potential but the very capacity of God Himself, the fullness of His holiness. The grand lesson within the covenant of the law is sealed with the words of Lord Jesus when He says, "humanly speaking it is impossible, but with God all things are possible", (**Matthew 19:26**). God's journey to the birth of light begins with Abraham, a faithful servant to symbolize the covenant of faith rather than works, holiness rather than good deeds. By his faith, a son was born not by the strength of man but in the frailness of humanity, in the barrenness of our nature, after the exhaustion of our strength. The fundamental principle within the first covenant is seen when Moses parts the Red sea, when Joshua and Israel break down the walls of Jericho, it is seen in the might of Samson, the greatness of David and the words of the prophets. The principle is that alone we can do nothing, but with God even the dead can be brought back to life. Genesis shows the futility of the first covenant between humankind and God as God shows through His covenant with Abraham that faith would conquer works just like in creation He sealed that dark and light could not mix as good would produce good and evil would produce evil. Thus with Abel dead and the seed within Cain reproducing, it was within Seth that God would bring to pass His marvellous plan of life. Yet first He had a lesson He had to teach humanity, that greater than their sin was their death, that deeper than their quest for the purpose of life was its very futility. He had to show He would come and become a light that cannot be engulfed by darkness. Through Moses the laws were established, laws that were meant to keep Israel holy for in her was the seed of promise. In many stipulated rules and regulations, God revealed His light to humanity, absolute righteousness. Israel, surrounded by a dark world would serve as God's herald of light as said by the Lord Jesus, "you know very little about the One you worship because salvation comes through the Jews", (**John 4:22**) The whole world had a basic idea that all that was; came from somewhere, thus within the confines of their darkness they allowed that darkness to guide them through the dark passage of life. Amidst this, God rescues Israel from Egypt and in so doing He shows humanity that He is the **I AM.** Yet despite knowing this Israel could not follow Him for the sole reason that light and darkness could not mix. Hence again, the seed of Cain naturally hated what it had despised from the very start, light. God is absolute light but because

Israel was blind she could not see this. If anything this is the message emanating from the covenant of the law, that God is life and life alone, that wishing to follow Him, humanity could not because of the power of death that bound us. It is the power we ate in the very start and not having God's image we could not follow Him. Israel was like those who look at a mirror towards a vision of perfection which they were meant to emulate yet by nature it was impossible because human nature is dark and the nature of God is light and according to the laws of nature we separate light from darkness. It has already been established that every tree produces fruit of its kind and our capacity to produce good had died away with Abel.

The message given through the law is that the rift that separates us from God is so great that even slightest things could defile us in the sight of God making us ceremonially unclean. Under the covenant of the law, man had to eat certain things, cleanse themselves a certain way, for this time and even after they did all that, they were always at the risk of God's anger if they broke any of the laws and regulations. Basically it was impossible to pursue the law that's to be right with God. To the seeds He had planted God said be fruitful and multiply, yet one seed died and one multiplied to produce not only a harvest of sin but death and with death came blindness, sickness, spiritual darkness, thirst and hunger. With the introduction of the Jewish law was born a struggle between knowledge and nature. Human nature was sinful and the knowledge man was that of the difference between right and wrong. Yet since God is the only light, the light that man's nature separated him from he staggered in the vast darkness of sin and desolation. Mankind became slaves to sin, imprisoned within the high walls of darkness, sin and death. God had to walk with Israel through this path so that what was to come next would truly be light and not only that, but it would be a spring of bubbling water never to run dry.

The Covenant of Life

Genesis 4:25, "God has granted me another son in place of Abel, who Cain killed." In the scriptures we are told this of Seth, that in likeness he resembled his father Adam and Adam in the account of the genealogy is the Son of God. The covenant of law has taught us that to exist is not to live. King Solomon concludes in his old age, having tried everything under the sun, that everything is meaningless. God had granted him great wisdom and he was the wisest man to ever live but his concluding words are "meaningless, everything is meaningless".

Yet God had given a son to Eve, a son to replace Abel the seed of goodness, a seed that would see its preservation through Noah, a light to shine in Abraham, a light called Israel. In the book of Revelations chapter 19 we are told of a rider on a white horse whose title is the **Word of God,** whose robes are dipped in wine, blood of wine. He is the Word of God, the One by which all men shall live by. He is the Word that Jesus tells us to part, eat and His blood that we must drink for out of Him Flows Rivers of living water. As already seen in the Garden of Eden, the seed that had been born within humanity could not endure eternity, for it was death. So in front of the tree of life was placed a two edged sword, the sword which resembled the Word of God, the very Word which was the way to eternal life. The message of Jesus is not a message of goodness alone but it is the message of life through faith.

Human nature is death, which is the child of darkness and this is the great rift that separated man from God and life itself for God still had a veil. Under the first covenant He had revealed the futility of human efforts as required by the law that said be "holy as God is holy." How was it that from a barren tree God would expect fruit? Job's friend Eliphaz sums it up neatly when he says, "in the silence I heard a voice...can a mortal be innocent before God? Can anyone be pure before the Creator?" (**Job 4:17**). Under the law humanity was as God had said long ago, "I will curse the land, no longer will the ground yield good crops for you, no matter how hard you work" and "from now on you will be a homeless wanderer on earth", (**Genesis 4:12**). Humanity toiled on the ground trying to produce goodness for God but naturally producing bitter fruit and enticing the anger of God. The child of sin is death but the gift of God is eternal life through Jesus Christ. The law was keeping humanity as the Lord unfolded His plan of salvation that is later revealed as God's original plan. God knew the consequences of human nature from the start, but He had to reveal His heart to man, to let us know that it is not by our goodness nor is it by our works but it is by God's grace that we find salvation.

"Whoever looks upon the bronze snake shall be saved," (**Numbers 21:8**). Whoever looks upon the Son of Man shall be saved from death and the curse of barrenness. Jesus said in the account of the gospel according to (**John 5:39**), "you look upon the scriptures thinking they will give you life but the scriptures point to me". Jesus is life itself, He is God himself robed in the flesh He created. He is the light humanity lost when Adam and Eve fell, yet in Seth, He is the seed that is reserved, the risen Abel, the hope and the promise of life. He is the two edged sword placed before the tree of eternal life, the sword that would conquer Cain and his death. It is only through Him that man can get to taste eternity with God. It is of Him that Samson testifies when he says, "Out of the eater came something to eat. Out of the strong came something sweet," (**Judges 14 v 14**). For it is Jesus, the Lion of Judah who is sacrificed for the sins of the world and out of Him came the promise of better things just like the lion Samson killed and out of whom he found honey. Under the covenant of life, we are not only able to do good deeds, but we are given the right to become children of God.

Whilst the seed of darkness multiplied and filled the world, God would preserve the seed of light through the reincarnated Abel, Seth. Through Noah, God cleansed the world of evil in the first baptism. God begins the new world through the descendants of Seth and Abraham finds favour with God because of his faith, and that's where the covenant of life begins. We have already established that there are two covenants, the first covenant of the law and the second, of life. When God establishes the covenant family, He begins to tell a story that would come together with the coming One. He weaves a tapestry that He would eventually present to all creation at the cross. God tells His epic tale through Ishmael and Isaac, that it is not by our effort but by the Spirit of the Sovereign Lord that creation is made whole. Isaac father's twins with Rebecca, and just as Esau sold his birth right to Jacob, so did the death sell its right over God's people to Jesus at the cross. This was God's promise of freedom from the curse and the law. God testifies of Jesus through Rachael and Leah. Leah was the wife of the birth right and Rachael was that of desire. So, just as Jacob got the wife he did not want and had to toil for 14 years in total to get the one he wanted, so it was with mankind cursed to live under the rule of darkness and sin as well as under the rule of an impossible law. Yet just as Jacob finally got the wife he wanted so mankind found rest at the cross. God testifies of Jesus through Tamar, when all her efforts of reproduction had failed and all her lawful ways of getting married had failed her, it was by cunning chance that she finally produced a male line of Judah. So God shows how human effort under the first covenant would give way to the second covenant of faith. He also shows how human nature and its barrenness would be replaced by life. The message resounds in Zerah and Perez, for although Zerah was to gain the inheritance of the first born, it is upon the heel of Perez that the scarlet string is tied and if we read further we discover that Perez is the direct ancestor of King David, the king chosen by God himself, the promise of the kingdom of God. So through the covenant family God establishes the promise of faith conquering works and life conquering death. The first born sons in the covenant family gave their inheritance to the second born sons, revealing how the first covenant of the law would be replaced by that of life and how darkness would be conquered by light. So we the vultures, the beasts of prey scavenging in our fruitless efforts, like the vultures in the baker's dream, are fed by the impaled body of Christ, the bread of life. Yet even though the body is impaled, the blood is served as an ever quenching wine. This is the enduring message God brings forth through the dreams of the baker and the wine bearer. Like the sons of Joseph, though humanity was conceived in Egypt {the depth of sin}, it is given the right to become children of Israel, God's own special possession. This is the message of Genesis, that the first will give way for the second. The era that was to come was to show that it is only through God that we are made whole. So mankind experienced its right of birth, which is barrenness, but in the darkness a light would shine, the sworn Prince to the eternal throne the One we would sell our right of birth to.

Within the law God, teaches us the impossibility of breaking our yokes, for although Moses wished to free his fellow Israelites, he could not do it by his might but by the spirit of the Sovereign Lord who descended to him in the burning bush as a fire that does not destroy but sanctifies. "*The Spirit of the Sovereign Lord is upon me, for the lord has anointed me to proclaim that the captives shall be set free*" (**Isaiah 61:1**). A Saviour came to Israel to lift her out of the yoke of slavery. By the waters that engulfed others, Moses was lifted up symbolizing how he would lift Israel out of bondage. Moses also testifies of Jesus the Saviour as Israel was saved from the angel of death by the blood of the lamb, in the same way God offered Himself as a lamb to humanity, as a ransom for our sin and the consequences of death. Our Saviour is the unleavened bread, His word and flesh is to be consumed with no alteration. His word is pure, undefiled and abundant life, He is the lamb sacrificed to set humanity free as stipulated by the law.

In the Tabernacle it is Him we see surrounded by a curtain of sorrow, passion and blood, yet living within the hearts of stone. A cloud tower is our Lord, a fire burning with passion to lead His people out of barrenness. Moses witnesses to Jesus the Messiah as he lifts up the staff and parts the Red sea, yes, humanly speaking it is impossible but with God all things are possible. Through the law Moses reveals the glory of God, an image of perfect holiness, life and light. He is the living manna that sustains all who trust in Him, the bread from heaven to feed mankind in the desert land he calls home. He is the rock from which living water flows, a water to quench humanity's thirst. David testifies of Jesus as the living water poured out for humanity when he is offered water from the well of Bethlehem by his mighty men and he says as he poured it out to the Lord, *"Far be it from me, O Lord to do this... Is it not the blood of men who went at the risk of their lives,"* (**2 Samuel 23:17**). Likewise through the psalmist Jesus says, *"I am poured out like water all my bones are out of joint,"* (**Psalms 22:14**).

The words of God still resound in the wilderness, if you eat from this tree you will surely die. Confronted by pure light, Israel was blinded by God's light and could not see her death. The fruit from the seed we ate long ago would remain within humanity causing him to sin against God. These are the concluding words of God to the group of Israelites that had left Egypt with him, *"You will never enter my place of rest,"* (**Hebrews 4:3**) This is the message that God had given through Esau and Jacob, the one he had given through Perez and Zerah; human effort is futile and barren. Abraham wished to produce a son for God through Hagar but God was not pleased, for it is not by works but by faith that humanity is made whole. Efforts of work could not please God just like the offering of Cain could not. Under the law, humanity works to gain by effort what can only be gained by grace. That's why after entering the land of promise, Israel would continue to fail God because of their inner death. The seed within man was death naturally, it was attracted to the death amongst the pagan nations. Like yeast, the evil of the pagan nations soon grew to conquer the goodness that God had stipulated in the law. So it was sealed, the futility of human effort in meeting God's law. The witnesses of Lord Jesus would come to save Israel from the clutches of their enemies gaining peace for only forty years and falling once more to the will of their birth right; death and failure.

When His body is impaled, His blood shall endure to be served as a quenching wine pleasing to the soul making man everlasting. God is the light and the life. He is the source of life and He testifies of Himself and Christ through Israel. In that hour when the star appeared we sold, our birth right to its rightful heir. Though the sceptre of rulership did not depart from Judah, the kings of that house produced nothing of it, but there came a king riding on a donkey and He was the I AM.

Jesus as testified in the gospel of John is the bread of life. He is given to man as the living water. In His own words in **John 2:19-21**, He is the One who is greater than the temple. Break down the temple which is His body, He says and in three days I will raise it up. In the midst of barrenness and death, He offers to law His covenant of glorious exchange. His promise is to give us life and the eternity we lost in the beginning of time. But we know it has already been established that there is no eternity without goodness. Israel's journey has already shown that man can never be righteous by works, yet Jesus offers humanity the righteousness of God, for what? **For His Death.** It is an exchange that is unbelievable that God who through Isaiah testifies that I have no equal, who says that He holds the earth like a grain of sand within His hands. The eternal, Living One who is robed in the universe clothed Himself in flesh and blood to die so that when we chose to look to Him and die to our death we could live forever in Him.

Light and darkness: when darkness consumed man, humanity lost the right to be called children of God. The very essence of the gospel is not that God wants to be pleased with our good works and piousness. What He wants for humanity is what we lost in ignorance; **life.** Deeper than heaven is a life shared and lived with the One who created us. Yet true life can only be found in God, who alone is holy. Throughout the scriptures God calls out to us to sell our birth right to Him for out of Him Flows Rivers of living water that will quench our deepest thirst for purpose, for peace, and life. When you drink from me you will never thirst again, He promises. So Jesus the Creator of all things, chooses to be impaled so that when He dies, the power of sin and death would perish, for unlike all had entered the place of death, He alone was born of the Spirit and not of man. His name which is above all things above the earth and below the heavens conquered death and when He was resurrected all humanity rose with him, for death had lost its sting. When the dead heard the **Word of God** and a light shone in the darkness, He dressed their dry bones with flesh and gave His blood as their life blood and from the living waters that He is, they drank and lived. I am the resurrection and the life. As He commanded death to leave Lazarus, so will God do for all who believe in Him.

We know, says the blind man whose sight was restored by Jesus, that since the beginning of time no one has ever healed a person born blind. We know that since the beginning of time no one has ever lifted the curse of death from humanity. Jesus healed the woman struggling with the issue of blood, those cast into unending isolation by the law, by His love Jesus set humanity free. He set Mary Magdalene, a woman destined by the law to die, telling the Pharisees to look carefully and judge wisely, the dilemma is the same: humanity is born dead. As the Apostle Paul states anyone born of the seed of Eve is born a sinner, and meaning anyone born on earth is born barren and dead. Yet our Lord Jesus is born by the Spirit not under the curse of Cain but above it. He is the abundance of life who walks on water; the path to our salvation and calms the raging seas; the shout of death. The very Word of God revealed to man is the resurrection and the life. When we have toiled and are tired Jesus gives us His wine, the fulfilment of the law which is His blood and humanity testifies; why have you brought the best for last?

Upon the cross when our God is given sour wine, out of Him flowed water, and life. If only you knew the gift God has for you, you would ask me for living water and I would give it, our Lord says. Jesus makes humanity whole, not because we deserve it but because it pleases

Him. Behold the Lamb of God that takes away the sins of the world; the glorious covenant of life, when God gave His life to defeat death and the power of sin. Jesus feeds the 5000 with His body and His message is that I AM more than enough to fill your everlasting hunger. The water that flows Him as the Rock does not just quench a physical thirst, but a spiritual thirst for life. And His blood is not the kind that washes away sin for a day but it washes away our sin and allows us to be called children of God.

Under the eternal covenant of life and recreation, God offers Himself as the risen Abel, the firstborn of a new creation. He offers Himself as the two edged sword that will part open the Red Sea and allow us entrance to God's resting place and to the tree of eternal life. This is the story of God and His people, the story of recreation through a covenant of blood and life which covers humanity's sin and shame for eternity just as the first death of the lamb in the Garden of Eden covered the shame of Adam and Eve.

EXODUS

T he book of Exodus tells the tale of the exit of the people of Israel from the land of Egypt. The tale of Israel and Egypt is a metaphorical symbolism that foretells God's desires and designs for His people. The symbolism must be understood in line of the two nations here mentioned. Israel, the children of Abraham are God's chosen people, His promise to His friend, Abraham. Egypt on the other hand is the symbol of the world and all its attributes. It is a land filled with sin and corruption, at its figurehead is Pharaoh, the vicious slave driver. The book of Exodus can be divided into three parts according to the different themes:

♣ The first part is a revelation of truth and salvation.

♣ It shows to us God as the only God, as the mighty One who redeems and saves.

♣ The second part shows to us the heart of God.

Having released Israel from the land of Egypt, having released Israel from the land of captivity, God reveals that to belong to Him reaches deeper than a physical freedom. His proclamation of freedom is man free from himself. He wishes to defy something within man so that the people may be His holy people; a blessing far deeper than physical freedom.

♣ The third part reveals that there is something within man that separates man from God: sin.

♣ A part that God builds the Tabernacle for-a place of meeting between God and man. It is in the Tabernacle that God will make His people holy. From this, we learn that true liberty to God is truth; a truth that set apart Israel from the world. It is the fulfilment of a new covenant between God and man and its requirements complete human liberty; be holy as I am holy is God's righteous command.

It is important to first understand the state of humanity, a state that had prompted God to destroy Sodom and Gomorrah. It is the state of sin that would always separate man from God. It is this state that at this stage of His journey God wishes not only to abolish, but to emphasize. He wishes to guide, inform and instruct. It is sin that God is responding to and it is sin that He aims to abolish. And how does God first reveal sin? Slavery. It is no coincidence that Israel is in slavery. It is important to note that intrinsically there is nothing that separates Israel from Egypt except the fact that they are God's chosen people, descendants of Abraham and the children of the promise. It is in this that we must address Israel in the first part; they are the Lord's special possession, set apart for His special will. And what is this will? It is to set them free from slavery. This is the foundation of God's relationship with Israel; they are slaves to be set free. Moses is God's chosen servant; His voice to the people, foreshadowing the promised Messiah. Pharaoh's daughter named him Moses; she explains "I lifted him out of the water." He is the last from a slain generation. It is Moses that God calls out of Egypt, an Israelite bound to Egyptian prince-hood. God shows his mercy to the displaced Israelite not only for his sake, but for all his people. Out of the burning bush He says to Moses, *"I have certainly seen the oppression of my people in Egypt. I have heard their cries of distress because of their harsh slave drivers. Yes I am aware of their suffering. So I have come down to rescue them from the power of the Egyptians and lead them out of Egypt into their own fertile and spacious land. It is a land flowing with milk and honey- the land where the Canaanites, Hittites, Amorites, Perizzites, Hivites and Jebusites now live. Look the cry of the people of Israel has reached me and I have seen how harshly the Egyptians abuse them. Now go, for I am sending you to Pharaoh. You must lead my people out of*

Egypt." This is the Lord's great proclamation to the person He sends. It is a two part mission upon which Moses embarks. Israel is to be uprooted and replanted, where she is to be replanted she is to supplant. Whilst she is sent out of Egypt, she is to supplant the Canaanites, Hittites, Amorites, Perizzites, Hivites and Jebusites. These people are likened to Egypt a symbol of human nature that has no place in God's plans. Before leaving for Egypt, Moses' son is to be circumcised upon God's command. Now you are a bridegroom of blood to me; indeed this is the union that God wishes to establish with His people a holy matrimony, a bond formed by blood. So this circumcision is a symbol of a separation of man from himself; a separation that will in turn bring union between man and God. It is the same union Christ promises and gives to His church. In this part Christ shows that He alone is God, greater than the makeshift powers that constitute the hierarchy of Egypt both politically and spiritually. God reveals Himself to Moses as Yahweh; in power He came to His people to free them from Egypt; from human slavery to sin.

It is the union of Israel and Egypt that is at the heart of this study. It is a union that will be broken; a perfect circumcision completed by Christ, the bridegroom of blood. That is His purpose to circumcise the holy from the unholy, to set apart the light from the darkness. God proclaims that He would show His wonderful power through Pharaoh and it is for this purpose that God hardens his heart. It is through this that God shows both Israel and Egypt that only He is God. Egypt is a symbol of the captor of man, of the death that holds man hostage; it is a slave driver without which Israel would not be slave. Therefore Egypt is sin itself and it is from sin that God aims to circumcise His people. By understanding the slavery of Israel to Egypt we are called to understand our own slavery to sin. If not for God's mercy, Israel would have remained in slavery forever. Egypt is an institution, a royal dynasty showing within its framework all the strongholds of human nature: a vicious leader, an unjust system, a worship of revered idols, and a strong economy whose linchpin is slave labour. It is at the height of Egyptian power that God displays His power, showing both man and the institution he is under that He alone is I AM.

What started to Egyptian sorcerers as a contest soon becomes the downfall of the great and proud empire leading Jethro to confess, "I know now that the Lord is greater than all other gods because He rescued His people from the oppression of the proud Egyptians", **(Exodus 18:11)**. The nine plagues that came ushered the downfall of Egypt, yet it is on the tenth that God seals the defeat. He kills the first born children of Egypt both humans and animals. God has triumphed over the Egyptian heir, the crown prince thus the future ruler of Egypt. He cuts off the dynasty and the institution. Here we must look back at the covenant family. We know that God has denounced the first born son for the second, He has promised to cut down human nature for His holiness. Here we see the first born, the symbol of the first nature (sin) dead. It is laid down to bring forth the true son-ship that God desired, the children of the covenant who are set apart for God's holiness. This is the Passover, "it is Passover sacrifice to the Lord for He passed over the houses of the Israelites in Egypt. And though He struck the Egyptians He passed our families", **(Exodus 12:27)**. This is the great salvation, the Passover told here as "the day to remember forever, the day you left Egypt the place of your slavery", **(Exodus 13:3)**. A foreshadow of a time to come when all humanity would be saved from slavery to sin.

The book of exodus is of an exit and a defeat. It is Israel's exit from Egypt, and Egypt's downfall. Israel is saved and thus redeemed, but it is not only for a demonstration of power that Pharaoh is destroyed. It is to show God's justice and the power of His salvation. Upon leaving Egypt God tells Moses *"divide the water so the Israelites can walk through the middle of the sea on dry ground"*, **(Exodus 14:16)**. So Moses does as God has commanded, raising his hand over the sea and the Lord parts the waters by a strong east wind and a path is made for God's chosen people to pass through. It is as the Lord Jesus says later on that *"humanly speaking it is impossible but with God all things are possible", (Matthew 19:26).* It is by love that we the people are saved, not only has Israel done nothing to deserve this but primarily the mode of their exit is absolutely sublime. Thus as they march out, we hear Christ praised as the Messiah, *"Your right hand, O Lord is glorious in power. Your right hand O Lord smashes the enemy. In the greatness of Your majesty You overthrow those who rise against You. At the blast of your breath the waters piled up... who is like You among the gods O Lord, glorious in holiness, awesome in splendour, performing great wonders? You raised your hand and the earth swallowed our enemies. With Your unfailing love You lead the people You have redeemed. In Your might, you guide them to Your sacred home...the power of Your arm makes them lifeless as stone...until the people You purchased pass by", (Exodus 15).* This is the purpose of Israel's salvation; that they may be brought back from death to life. It is God's righteous plan that at the end of His salvation mission all creation proclaims Him to be the One worthy of eternal rule. It is God as Christ being proclaimed all the way through; it is His mighty right hand that makes the circumcision possible. Thus by this strong east wind, Israel is ransomed from death to life. It is for this reason by this way that God saves Israel from slavery. It is all the way a plea for another kind of exit which was to fill another kind of void more intrinsic than extrinsic. *"The Egyptians you see today will never be seen again," (Exodus 14:13)* says the Lord. God's message is that He will destroy sin forever never to be seen again. It is sin and the institution here symbolized by Egypt that God proclaims He has set apart for disaster. *"My great glory will be displayed through Pharaoh and his troops, his chariots and charioteers. When my glory is displayed through them all Egypt will see my glory and know that I am the Lord"* (Exodus 14: 17-18), says the Lord.

The institution of Egypt is based on a foundation of lies and ideology, it is this empire founded upon ignorance that God wishes to enlighten and the basis of this enlightenment is the display of His great power. He does this by thrashing the heart of Egyptian power; the *Pharaoh and all the pillars of his power. At the end we read that, "of all the Egyptians who had chased the Israelites into the sea, not a single one survived." (Exodus 14:10)-'The power of Your right hand makes them lifeless as stone",* (**Exodus 15:16**) at the end of this journey we have a ransomed people and a vanquished slave driver. So God has accomplished the task He set out, He destroyed the Egyptian power and brought salvation unto the Israelites.

This takes us to the second part of the book where we will look at true freedom according to God. We have deduced that Israel was a slave to Egypt in the same way she was slave to sin. Having displayed His salvation power there is a path that means more to God than physical freedom. The purpose of humankind is to know God. There is something within humanity that God wishes to reveal, slavery that God understands as deeper than physical slavery. It is slavery less seen but more felt, its chains reaching deeper than the physical chains of human bondage. Therefore having saved Israel from the Egyptian institution, God wishes to form His own institution with Israel, and its framework are His standards. All laws address the reality of human society; all of them are based upon the situation of the subject people. This is not unlike God's law given to Moses. The only difference is that the Mosaic Law is not man-made; it does not dance to the tune of human nature. It is an institution meant to supplant the human institution still existent within the very makeup of the Israeli people. As noted before, nothing intrinsically separates the Jew from the Gentile or the Israelite from the Egyptian. It is not by chance that God decides to take the longer route to the Promised Land for the longer route is the narrow path. It has a double purpose here both literal and symbolic. The symbolism is that it reflects the condition of the human race; a condition of having lost God and the long struggle of finding our way back to Him either knowingly or unknowingly. To Israel a journey of eleven days took forty years, for it was God's will to teach Israel the only way to live. Later on we find God pleading with His people, *"O how I wish you could listen to my words and find life."* This is the basis of God's covenant with His people. It was a covenant of righteousness that was made on this special day; a covenant that promised God's friendship for Israel's love.

In the first covenant there are three festivals that God made in order to close the rift that existed between God's holiness and human sin. Now ransomed Israel is called upon to revisit the issue of their slavery only the state of the bondage is different. Israel is slave to the same slave master who was personified in Pharaoh, its institutions revealed in Egypt. Thus there is another exodus that needs to come to pass. This exodus is shown in the three festivals as well as the law given to the Israelites. Israel upon being given the law is elevated above the human race for they were chosen to know the one true God. In the process of covenant making, God wishes to destroy sin in humankind by showing that He is Lord glorious in power. Yet the glory of His power is the power of His holiness. It is this holiness that He intended to give His children. In order to do this He had to reveal the sin within people. Before revealing the law to the people God had something to teach ignorant Israel, clothed in human nature. It is a lesson to all humanity that teaches us to understand the bridge that God aims to build; a bridge from death to life. God goes about the lesson by revealing the state of human nature. The human condition is Marah, the bitter waters that the Israelites found in the desert of Shur. Yet out of this God gives them good water to drink. He replaces sour water with pure water. This is the divide God wishes us to understand when we are introduced to His salvation. Human nature is Marah but it is God's good will that after this, humanity finds abundant water on the oasis of Elim. This is where the Israelites found 12 streams and 70 palm trees.

Humankind is by nature unable to identify with God because of this quality the Israelites yearn for Egypt and its vile pleasures as symbolized by their yearning for Egyptian meat and bread. Yet God does not grant them the desires of their heart instead He gives them food more fulfilling than Egyptian bread and meat. This is the Lord's response to their hunger, *"look I am going to rain down food from heaven for you,"* **(Exodus 16:4).** This food called manna because of its foreign nature fulfils Israel's hunger in the wilderness. To sum it up God says, *"By evening you will realize it was the Lord who brought you out of the land of Egypt. In the morning you will see the glory of the Lord, because He has heard your complaints... in the evening you will have meat to eat and in the morning you will have all the bread you want. Then you will know that I am the Lord your God,"* **(Exodus 6).** To draw an analogy, at the Red Sea it is written, *"The cloud settled between the Egyptian and Israelite camps. As darkness fell, the cloud turned to fire, lighting up the night...but just before dawn the Lord looked down on the Egyptian army,"* **(Exodus 14).** The first analogy is in reference to the bread; the bread for which at Marah God tested the Israelites when He said, *"If you will listen to the voice of the Lord your God and do what is right in His sight, obeying His commands and keeping all His decrees, then I will not make you suffer any of the diseases I sent on the Egyptians for I am the Lord who heals you,"* **(Exodus 15:26).** Jesus says I am the bread of heaven and we know that His flesh is true meat. He is the bread that came down from heaven offered to anyone who desires life. He is both the evening and morning sacrifice. God says, in the evening you will know that I am the Lord who rescued you from Egypt and on that same night you will have meat to eat. This meat that reveals God to us is the body of Christ. Upon seeing Jesus on the cross the Roman soldier says, *"Indeed he was the Son of God,"* **(Matthew 27:54).** By morning you will have plenty of bread which will show the glory of God and this is the body of Christ offered to all who believe. The same bread is the Word of which God says, *"For man shall not live by bread alone but by every word that proceeds from the mouth of God,"* **(Matthew 4:4).** This is the true life that God offers, the great divide between Marah and the good water is the manna, the Word of God that makes us right with Him. It is in darkness that we see God alight yet when His word lives in us we are circumcised from Egypt: sin and thus recreated by the Eternal Word: Christ. This is the covenant, the foundation of God's relationship with Israel. It is sealed when God offers thirsty Israel water from the rock. In the wilderness we find a barren people given food by God, a food He writes down within the law and it is the law itself that is the revelation of God's life and truth; the one that if Israel follows she would be free indeed. Moses names his son Geshom, *"I have been a foreigner in a foreign land,"* (**Exodus 2:22**) revealing how foreign those set apart for God are in this world of sin. His second son is named Eliezer for he said, *"The God of my ancestors was my helper; He rescued me from the sword of Pharaoh,"* (**Exodus 18:4**).It is God that takes us away from the foreign land into His promised land.

The Israelites travel for forty years in the wilderness so as to realize that God's Promised Land is not a physical place of rest but one that is spiritual. It does not command a physical exodus but one from within. At the heart of the law we have been given three festivals; namely The Festival of the unleavened bread, the festival of the first harvest and the festival of the final harvest. All of these when properly completed declare us as God's ransomed children. Yet we are called to look at the law, the proclamation of truth that God makes to barren Israel and to the human race. The law is a response to the nature of mankind by God. It is a step away from human natural sin towards the realization of truth that makes us right with God. God's relationship with Israel as, we have seen, is that of a God desiring salvation for His people. Saved Israel is being led to realize true salvation and true liberty. The covenant of the law starts with this, *"You know how I carried you on eagles' wings and brought you to myself. Now if you will obey me and keep my covenant you will be my own special treasure from among all the peoples on earth, for all the earth belongs to me. And you will be my kingdom of priests, my holy kingdom,"* (**Exodus 19:4-6**).It is God who is all Holy reaching down to humanity which is in need of circumcision and consecration. That is why before they are to meet with the Lord, Moses is given instruction to consecrate them and have them wash their clothing, abstain from sexual intercourse. Even after this they are declared not clean enough to approach the mountain of the Lord or else they would surely die. The law wishes to close he rift existing between humanity and God. To a people of nature, God prescribes a set of laws to guide their path so that the pursuit of the law can make them right with Him. The Mosaic Law is superior to all other laws because it is God's advocacy; the God who lost His children and declares their ways to be worthy of destruction. He reaches down to them out of mercy to forgive their sin and lead them towards His path. If the law accomplishes its task among God's people they will become His harvest. The law according to the rules of the unleavened bread, is to be taken as bread without yeast. Its purpose is to give people rest from their works as the Sabbath proclaims. Whilst in the wilderness God shows Israel a way out of an even greater wilderness than that before them; water better than what they were accustomed to was given to them at Shur; bread more fulfilling than manna. It is indeed the Word of God which is life giving. The law is the divide between ignorance and truth, between wandering and rest. Israel goes through an enlightenment meant to alter all history. God reaches down to Israel so they may herald the truth unknown to the human race. It is a truth as scarce as water in a desert and it can be proven so in the case of human existence. The Ten Commandments reveal that there is only one God; that any other gods made in the image of anything are idols and the curse procured by worship of them will last for generations. The commandments teach humanity to honour the name of the one true God, to honour the Sabbath day which will be revealed later as the day humankind was recreated by God through Christ. There is a call to honour parents, a call to abstain from murder, adultery, theft, false testimony and covetous behaviour. The law scrutinizes humankind, analyses them and wishes not only to reveal human nature but also to teach humanity to abstain from the inclinations of their nature.

Moses splatters blood upon the people and says, *"Look this blood confirms the covenant the Lord has made with you in giving you these instructions,"* (**Exodus 24:8**). That covenant is the promise of a true exodus, the living blood that would cast the Egypt living within Israel out of God's people in the same way God set Israel free from Egypt. For there is an inner Egypt in all of humankind as in Israel and it is from that slavery that God embarks to save His lost children. This salvation is seen to come from the word of God; the truth found in the law and its life found in the living Word of God; Christ. If anything this is the prime message of Exodus; that Israel is slave to sin as she is slave to Egypt. Only the holiness of God can make her holy; this is the truth that would be the prime foundation of God's relationship with the people of Israel at the same time the basis upon which He would seek after the earth.

LEVITICUS

T

he history of the Jews has been directed by God and in its early stages, it was the teaching of a creation of the nature of God. At the heart of this education was the Levitical Priesthood. It was at the heart and centre of Jewish society, politics, judiciary and economy. It has been given to us in understanding that God upon saving Israel from bondage in Egypt, meant to illustrate bondage even greater than a physical slavery to a physical slave master. Israel had been saved by Moses through might from Egypt yet Israel remained in the place of slavery but to a different slave master. Israel was slave to sin, tainted by the dirt of ungodliness that separated her from God. It is for this reason that God raises up an order of advocates to stand between humanity and God serving the supreme purpose of purifying the people making them right with God. God says this of the priests, *"They must be set apart as holy to their God and must never bring shame on the name of God,"* (**Leviticus 21:6**).

The Levitical priests are the symbol of Israelite holiness; made holy by God in order to purify His people. They were set apart to meet the perfection of God. They were not allowed to marry prostitutes, divorced women, they were not allowed to touch the dead body of a relative, shave their heads, trim their beards or cut their bodies. At the head of the priesthood was the High Priest who had the special task of carrying upon him the sins of the people. He was not allowed to leave his hair uncombed, tear his clothing, to go near a dead body, or leave the sanctuary of the lord to attend to a dead body. He was to marry only a virgin from his own clan. No descendant of the priests with defect qualified to offer food to his God, this would defile the holy places.

The priests were meant to serve as both advocates and the standard; advocates of the people to God and a standard of God to the people. The priest served as the purifier of the people; he stood in the place of God. He was taken out from the common men and through the process of ordination was qualified to make holy the unholy and just the unjust. The priest was the instrument of God to perform the exodus he had always desired and to distinguish between, "what is sacred and what is common. What is ceremoniously unclean and what is clean and... teach the Israelites all the decrees that the Lord has given through Moses," (**Leviticus 10:10**).

The priest is purified by God but he is not himself pure. In fact the first High Priest is Aaron; the helper of Israel in building the golden calf. Nothing exists within this man in his raw state that qualifies him to be priest. It is for this reason that purification is performed through a series of offerings. So the priest is not a priest until he is purified. The purity that the priests represent is not their purity but it belongs to the Pure One; He who purifies the Tabernacle and alter, He who makes the bulls and declares them pure for the purification. It is 'Purity' that rests at the heart of the construction of the Jewish religion. Israel is called to be God's herald and it is Aaron and the order he represents that is tasked with purifying this herald so she can send the message well. Israel was meant to be perfected and it was not just the perfection of being law abiding but of being a people born of the law itself. Israel was meant to be cleansed in a ceremony alien to that of other nations; she was to be cleansed by the purity of God Himself. Here stood an advocate created by God for the sole purpose of achieving this purpose. Yet the weakness that rested within the priest was human weakness; a weakness that if realized would lead to death. "This is a permanent law for you, to purify the people of Israel from their sins making them right with the Lord once each year," (**Leviticus 16:34**). God's perfection would be realized amongst the people in this way.

The Atonements

There is an awakening made within the heart of the Israelite, a self-awakening not witnessed with rest of humanity. It is humanity's sinful nature that prompts God to create the law. It is this sin within that God wants humanity to step away from, it needs annihilation. The path that Israel is led to as a child is a path towards the Father's heart. God's ultimate desire is that His people may be holy as He is holy. The unity He seeks with His people is more than the physical unity of a people who see God at Mount Sinai; the stepping away is more than the people who step out of Egypt. There is something within humanity that must die and it's for this reason that the atonements are introduced to the Jewish religious institution. Mankind is by nature guilty and defiled therefore for this reason born in need of God's forgiveness. To check the state of His people, God makes for them a solution of offerings whereby the holy would be given in place of the unholy. The animal used for the offering was a most holy offering and this animal stood in the place of the people before God, this sacrificed lamb is sacrificed in place of a people deserving of death. God says. "Lay your hand on the animal's head so the Lord may accept its death in your place to purify you, making you right with him," (**Leviticus 1:4**). The offerings for sin, peace and guilt carry with them the weight of humanity's transgressions at the same time they stand as purity to God, to purge these transgressions. The offerings are meant to sanctify the people before God therefore saving them from death.

The Levitical order is the beginning of Israel's vocation and through this order God would continuously remind His people of that which they were in need of. Yet as God's communication with this child of Abraham continues there is a feeling that this child gets; a feeling unlike that which she felt in Egypt. It is the feeling of being seen and analysed, yet she must awaken once more to that which is in her, that need for purification. God continues to weigh His people and as He does so His conclusion is 'Unclean'. There is something perpetually resounding in the ears of the ordinary Israelite. They hear words they have never heard before; they hear 'ceremoniously unclean and clean' and for the first time they are led to evaluate themselves in a way Egypt could never allow them to. The Israelite feels like a child being taught to talk yet she is an old woman being taught to speak the Hebrew tongue and at its heart is the word 'pure'. She feels as though all the Egyptian slag is being lifted up as she sits before Moses; God's lawgiver. As she listens to the laws she cannot help but feel the depth of her impurity. At the same time she feels the weight of God's holiness as she begins a journey which is a duty. She must awaken to realize that the offerings then spoken were made for one just as she.

Israel sits through this lecture as God begins to tell her that she is inclined to ungodliness. For the first time she feels that she has become herself and in those very moments she feels unity with her brothers and sisters and a pull away from the Egyptian once living within her; this is the purpose of God's pursuit. God has pursued Israel with success out of Egypt, now He must pull Egypt out of the Israelite. Human nature is at the centre of all this; God reveals the natural impurity of His people at the same time He reveals His own purity as the only one that can purify Israel and bring her closer to God. Israel is enlightened to that self-realization that is yet veiled from the world at large so that if and when Israel accomplishes her vocation, the rest of God's children will be enlightened by the Light that is a cloud to Israel in the day and a pillar of fire at night.

God has introduced into the heartland of His people a road to childhood and to the attaining of His Fatherhood. As Israel is freed from Egypt, she is born and she is called to childhood. As she is born as a child, she is to walk away from her former parentage. As she does this her heart must be awaken to who she is as a creation; and so begins the sacred path to purification. God teaches Israel the depth her nature's inclinations and the consequences thereof. At the same time He shows His child a way out. As unclean Israel is to bath in water, she must also walk through a cleansing of her thoughts; as she breaks down the walls of her defiled house so must she break down the walls of Egyptian thought and as a lamb is offered in her place, she too must kill her old heart and mind to attain the purity of God.

When immortality and mortality meet, when the traveller on earth and the eternal Father come as one; there is a moral question asked and an ethical awakening. Whilst the rest of the world goes through moral philosophy; Israel is shown the path to inner purity. She is to discipline herself in accordance to the law; as Israel is born she is to be born within the law. It is to be her foundation and identity as a nation. Israelite birth is the birth of a light to the world; that is God's design and as she is designed; it is the law that forges her into the image of perfection that God is crafting. As God crafts the Israelite sculpture, He makes law after law and Israel is led away from her place of sleep to that of awakening. Israel is made to realize her special place in the world; to hold the banner of God's righteousness and to be the heritage of the Living One.

This is God's instruction to the people, "I am the Lord your God so do not act like the people in Egypt, where you used to live, or like the people of Canaan where I am taking you," (**Leviticus 18:3**). Israel is awakened to realize the evil within her and that of the people that surround her, of the land she has left and of the land she is to supplant. As God uproots the evil of His people He also plants. Israel is led to realize her true Creator and led away from the lies of idols and she is led towards a righteous path. A seed is planted within Israel, a seed with the capacity to reshape her. It is the start of human enlightenment and as Israel is taught to walk away from the Egyptian lifestyle; to love her neighbour as herself, to honour, respect, not steal, to care for the poor and needy; in those moments she is taught to walk away from what she was born into. She is taught to follow the path of the Almighty for in His very words there is life. Truth had descended, spoken and instructed.

As Israel walks and listens, it is still questioned whether the pupil has mastered the lecture that started in Egypt. Yet there is One amongst all who knows where He is taking humanity. It is His wisdom that has made the plan; He is the One making the advocacy. He is the Great Awakener whose light floods the depths of our darkness. As He walks with humanity, He is the driving force to all these mysteries of purity, holiness and cleanliness; to law abiding and life. As He speaks to Israel, the sublimity of His words reveal that God has veiled that which must be unveiled. He has closed that which only He can truly comprehend. With time, Israel becomes more and more the herald; the middleman to the third person who watches and wonders but would soon see and realize the truth, the ends which she herself seeks whether consciously or otherwise. The law foreshadows the things to come, the ceremonial cleansings; a shadow of an even deeper everlasting purification by the Unblemished High Priest. They mark a time when God's holiness shall triumph over evil and through Israel He speaks of a time to come and the nature of that time. This is His advocacy.

There is a bridge that exists, marking the divide between life and death. The words of God are life and light. Leviticus shows the place of God's law amongst the people. God reveals to us who we are at the same time He shows who He is. Israel is pronounced born yet her birth transcends a physical birth of a physical people. It is forever intrinsic, always speaking of an image to be altered and an image to be attained. God speaks of the price of following Him, it is life and the wages of sin are death and destruction. Whilst God gives Israel a choice between life and death, He seals the eternal fate of all humanity within His sacred Hands. He marks the dividing line between life and death, prosperity and poverty, bounty and little, peace and havoc, fertility and barrenness. The words of God are revealed as the life by which Israel must live. This also must be the fate of the world. It is through Israel that we learn the blessing of obedience and the curse for disobedience. Deeper than this is human nature which is sinful nature. We learn the beauty of walking upon the path of the Lord and the call of our vocation to be holy as God is holy. This is the essence of the Jewish education.

HOUSE OF DAWN

R

oyal House of David, Royal House of David's heir, House of David's Lord, a gift from the Most High God; its Source and its Heir. Amen.

A long time ago God anointed a young man, David, to be king over all Israel. The covenant promise was such that David's royal house would last forever. This is God's promise to David, *"for when you die and are buried with your ancestors, I will raise up one of your descendants, your own offspring and I will make his kingdom strong...I will secure his royal line forever. Your house and your kingdom will continue before me for all time and your throne will be secure forever,"* (**2 Samuel 7**).This same heir is shown to the prophet Daniel who saw Him, the Son of Man being given power and authority and dominion over the whole earth and everything in it; over heaven and everything. He is shown as a Rock cut from heaven whose dynasty will take over all the dynasties of the world.

In the book of Samuel we find the first king of Israel, King Saul who God had anointed first. The house of Saul and the house of David stand parallel to each other, with the house of Saul representing the dynasties of this world of which God said, *"This is how a king will reign over you. The king will draft your sons and assign them to his chariots and his charioteers, making them run before his chariots. Some will be generals and captains in his army, some will be forced to plow in his fields and harvest his crops and some will make his weapons and chariot equipment. The king will take your daughters from you and force them to cook and bake and make perfumes..."* (**1 Samuel 8:11-18**). This stands in stark contrasts to the house of David of which God said, *"Out of the stump of David's family will grow a shoot- yes a new Branch bearing fruit from the old root. And the Spirit of the Lord will rest on Him, the Spirit of wisdom and understanding...He will give justice to the poor and make fair decisions for the exploited...In that day the heir to David's throne will be a* *banner of salvation to all the world,"* (**Isaiah 11**). It is the house of David that is the hope of God's future kingdom and everlasting peace for the world. It is God's message that the oppressive government of mankind will be replaced by God's government of justice and peace.

In the book of Kings we are shown the dual lines of rulership, the dynasties of Judah and Israel, a streak of rebellious kings who caused all of Israel to sin against God. Eventually the house of David falls, this means that the kingdom which God spoke of was more than physical dominance. The house of David is best understood as the successor to the human dynasty or rather the usurper to the human dynasties. King Nebuchadnezzar has a dream of a statue of a man with a head of gold, chest and arms of silver, belly and thighs of bronze, legs of iron and feet of a combination of iron and baked clay. This statue which the prophet Daniel explains represents the dynasties of the world struck and completely smashed by a rock cut by the hands of God from a mountain. The prophet Daniel explains, *"During the reigns of those kings, the God of heaven will set up a kingdom that will never be destroyed or conquered. It will crush all these kingdoms into nothingness and it will stand forever. That is the meaning of the rock cut off from the mountain..."* (**Daniel 2**). At the heart of King David's reign, is the symbolism that he portrays. His works foreshadow the dynasty to come.

One of King David's greatest triumphs is his conquest over Goliath; this is symbolic of how God and Christ would triumph over His enemies at the cross. King David was a mighty warrior and at the centre of his military prowess was at the age30. These were great warriors mighty in battle. Yet God's message is not about a physical battle resulting in physical conquest. The conquest by which God intended to found and maintain His house is a different kind. Throughout his reign, King David was in battle defeating all of Israel's enemies. In the end this is his legacy; this and his unparalleled love for God, a love which would inspire God's spirit within him to write a number of psalms. It is a different kind of scene we witness in the psalms yet its purpose is not unlike that of his military victories. In battle we see David the great warrior, in the psalms we see a poet proclaiming the righteousness of his Lord. The book of Psalms is a testament to God and His Messiah. It reveals God for who He is, His love for good, His mercy; the goodness of the law, His forgiveness of sin, His everlasting kingdom, His pain and suffering.

He is shown as the King of glory and as a lamenting King; lamenting for His people Israel, lamenting for earth. He is victor over His enemies yet His victory is over sin; an enemy whose battlefield is not physical and whose weapons are not sword and shield. Thus the house of David foreshadows the conquest of God's salvation and holiness over the forces of darkness. *"I am both the source and heir to David's throne"*, is Lord Jesus' confession in Revelations 22:16. This is Jacob's blessing to his son Judah, *"Judah is a young lion who has captured his prey. Like a lioness who dares rouse him. He washes his robes in wine, his clothes in blood of grapes, his eyes are darker than wine, his teeth are whiter than milk, he ties the colt of his donkey to a choice vine..."* (**Genesis 49**).The kingdom of God is won through the death of its King, His robes are coloured by His blood; that is His anointing, He is crowned with a crown of thorns and He is named King of the world upon a cross. In this way, He brings together all time past and future to find definition at the cross.

The house of David is built upon the union of the Kingship and the Priesthood. He is king and priest in the order of Milchizedeck. It is the very Milchizedeck who blessed Abraham, the patriarch of the Jewish nation from which the Lord's promised heir would come. Therefore the blessing of the kingdom of peace and justice was upon Abraham and it would manifest in the tribe of Judah, in the house of David, through the One who is the rider on the white horse. Of Him it is written, *"Then I saw heaven open and a white horse was standing there. Its rider was named Faithful and True for He judges fairly and wages a righteous war. His eyes were like flames of fire and on his head were many crowns. A name was written on him that no one understood except himself. He wore a robe dipped in blood and his title was the Word of God...on his robe at his thigh was written this title: King of all kings and Lord of all lords,"* (**Revelations 49**). The prophet Isaiah saw this of Him, *"a child is born to us; a son is given to us. The government will rest on his shoulders. And he will be called Wonderful Counsellor, Mighty God, Everlasting Father, and Prince of Peace. His government and its peace will never end. He will rule with fairness and justice from the throne of his ancestor David for all eternity,"* (**Isaiah 9**). He carries the kingdom on His shoulders just as He carried the cross and in the same way Samson fell and brought down more of his enemies upon his death, so too God's Messiah triumphed over His enemies upon His death, thus establishing His everlasting kingdom.

The covenant promise between God and David is two way. It was binding only if David and his descendants were loyal to God and followed His ways. Upon failing to keep this part of the covenant, God took away His hand of blessing from them. Yet it still remained binding to David. This means that there was another descendant who would remain faithful to God's decrees and govern the people with truth. The same descendant is Jesus, ensuring that dominion in the house of David was based on righteousness. A righteousness that He would give to His people. In this way, He defeats all of God's enemies.

The foundation of the house of David is Justice, Truth and Righteousness. The union between the kingdom and the priesthood ensures that the kingdom is founded upon righteousness. God's kingdom is the dawn of a new age. It is both a beginning and an end as the scriptures state, *"Who has done such a thing, uniting all the generations since the beginning of time,"* (**Isaiah 41:4**). God unites all people as part of His kingdom and subjects of His dynasty. All humanity is called together as one under one confession that they were once dead; but God's High Priest is their atonement. This is the foundation of God's house for when it comes it is the dawn of a whole new age, the House of Dawn.

SONG OF A BARREN WOMAN

"Sing, O childless woman, you who have never given birth! Break into loud and joyful song, O Jerusalem, you who have never been in labour; for the desolate woman now has more children than the woman who lives with her husband, says the Lord. -**Isaiah 54:1**

W

e are a barren field producing nothing, a dried fig tree cursed to remain without fruit; we are the desert that does not know the embrace of rain. We are the barren woman who does not know the pains of labour or the joy of children yet God smiled upon us and gave us life, heaven smiled and the desolate desert earth became a garden of bounty and life. This is God's covenant promise to His people, that the people He cursed to produce no good for Him would once more bear fruit pleasant to Him. Eve is the mother of barrenness; cursed to bear children of thorns and thistles, children destined to perish. Yet God has a plan to replenish the earth; to give her a new mother; a mother of fresh fruit and a bounty harvest. Yet this mother is a barren woman; for God's message is humanity will not and cannot produce the beautiful, holy and perfect on their own.

Sarah stands parallel to Eve; she is the matriarch of God's new creation. She gives birth to Isaac in her old age, symbolizing how humankind would be granted the power to produce holiness for God in the old age of humanity's life. She says, *"Who would have thought that I would give my husband a child in my old age, surely God is great,"* (**Genesis 21:7**). Sarah symbolizes a lost world remembered by God; by His grace mankind will till the barren land and produce fruit of the Spirit. She is the mother of God's new creation and upon her rests the blessing of life and not the curse of Eve. Upon her God cancelled the rights Eve had over God's creation and all those who believe in Christ are born not under the curse of Eve, but under the blessing of Sarah.

Rebecca too is barren, yet later on God grants her twins, to carry forth the covenant promise. It is God's will to show that it is His mighty hand that preserves the promise not human will. The children of the covenant promise are children of the Spirit, gifts of God and not the result of human passion or plan. Rebecca gives birth to Esau and Jacob symbolizing the two covenants God would make with His people; it is God's will that the first creation be subdued by the second. So Esau the 1st born gives his birth right to Jacob as is God's will for all creation; that Eve give up her children to Sarah. Rachael and Leah too symbolize the two covenants. Rachael is the wife of promise but Jacob works for seven years only to be given the woman he does not want. In the same way humankind had to live under sin and the law in which they could produce nothing. After fourteen years of labour Jacob is given Rachael the wife he desired. He is given the best for last; in the same way after much suffering under the law humanity was given Christ and His righteousness. Rachael the beloved wife is barren just like Sarah and Rebecca before her; the message is the same. It is only God who grants life and who fulfils His covenant. Tamar, the daughter in law of Judah moves from brother to brother unable to conceive any children. Disguising herself she manages to trick Judah into giving her children. Again God shows that it is by His grace that mankind gains salvation. Tamar gives birth to Perez and Zerah. *"While in labour, one of the babies reached out his hand. The midwife grabbed it and tied a scarlet string around the child's wrist, announcing, This one came out first." But then he pulled back his hand and out came his brother!..."* (**Genesis 38:27-29**). This too shows how the second covenant of grace is held back and that of the law takes precedence. Yet the scarlet string is our promise of the covenant of the promise of the blood that cleanses all creation. Hannah was a barren woman who lived with the constant taunts of her sister wife, Penninah. Seeing her suffering and humiliation God granted her a son, Samuel, who was to be the first kingmaker in Israel and God's servant and seer. *"Those who were well fed are now starving and those who were starving are now full. The childless woman now has 7 children and the woman with many children wastes away..."* (**1**

Samuel 2:5) is Hannah's prayer upon being granted a child. It is God's promise to barren earth, the promise of a child after years of barrenness.

The Moabite Ruth is a widowed woman, loyal and diligent. She is unable to have children by her husband before he dies and her marriage to Boaz redeems the family of Naomi from being closed. God shows Himself as the Redeemer, the One who makes ripe grapes out of withering vines. The promise of God to Judah would endure not because of human effort or wisdom but because of the grace of God. Upon the agreement of Boaz to marry Ruth and redeem her family name the elders said, *"May the Lord make this woman who is coming into your home like Rachael and Leah from whom all the nation of Israel descended. May you prosper in Ephrathah and be famous in Bethlehem. And may the Lord give you descendants by this woman who will be like those of our ancestor Perez; the son of Judah and Tamar,"* (**Ruth 4:11-12**). Upon the birth of Obed it is said, *"Praise the Lord who has now provided a redeemer for your family. May this child be famous in Israel. May he restore your youth and care for you in your old age; for he is the son of your daughter in law who loves you and has been better to you than 7 sons."* It is Obed who would be the grandfather of David and it is in David's line that Jesus was born. So God ensures that His promise to His people is carried forth by His Spirit. He redeems a falling family in the same way He redeems His creation.

The Lord gives Elizabeth a son in her old age and he is to be a prophet of God to pave way for the coming of the promised Messiah. Of him Zechariah says, *"And you my little son, will be called the prophet of the Most High because you will prepare the way for the Lord. You will tell his people how to find salvation through forgiveness of their sins; because of God's tender mercy the morning light from heaven is about to break upon us; to give light to those who sit in darkness and in the shadow of death and to guide us to the path of peace,"* (**Luke 1:76-79**). A child is born to the Virgin Mary; a child who is the hope of all creation. It is Him who has been foreshadowed since the beginning of creation.

He is the Hope of a new age; born of the Spirit and not of the seed of man. He is the completion of all of God's promises; it is Him who is the promise of life, the Son of promise. Of Him it is written, *"Praise the Lord, the God of Israel because he has visited and redeemed his people. He has sent us a mighty Saviour from the royal line of his servant David, just as he promised through his holy prophets long ago. Now we will be saved from our enemies and from all who hate us. He has been merciful to our ancestors by remembering his sacred covenant- the covenant he swore with an oath to our ancestor Abraham,"* (**Luke 1:68-74**). He seals God's eternal promise to His people. It is the hope of eternal life through grace and not human works. He grants children to the barren women to show us that it is only He who ensures His covenant promise shall be fulfilled. Those born of the Lord and His grace are children of the Spirit, the redeemed granted childhood through the power of God's righteous promise.

PART TWO

BEING

The Life of Christ concerns Him who, being the holiest among the mighty, and the mightiest among the holy, lifted with His pierced hand empires off their hinges, and turned the streams of centuries out of its channel, and still governs the ages.

Jean Paul Richter 1763-1825

To affirm that the Christian doctrine refers only to personal salvation and has no bearing upon state affairs is a great error. To say so is but to assert an audacious, groundless, most evident untruth, which a moment's serious reflection suffices to destroy.

Leo Tolstoy

Christ is the visible image of the invisible God. He existed before anything was created and is supreme over all creation, for through Him God created everything such as thrones, kingdoms, rulers and authorities in the unseen world. Everything was created through Him and for Him.

Colossians 1 v 15-1

INTRODUCTION

THE REMOVAL OF GOD FROM THE WORLD STAGE

I

n antiquity there was never a question as to whether God was part of both private and public life. God was providence; the source of rain and sunshine, at the same time He was believed to choose kings and to be the inspiration behind their laws. Religion played a central role in the social, political and economic life of almost all ancient societies and civilizations. Divinity was the linchpin of ancient society, it was almost impossible to define phenomena without incorporating religion in that definition. With the spread of Westernization and as a result of the irreligious foundations of the age of Enlightenment, reason took precedence over religion. No longer would it suffice to explain the world through God, no longer was it permissible to choose leaders based on divine calling. Intelligence would be measured by use of reason and not intuition, no longer would metaphysics be dualistic, there would only be the material world and the answers to all the world's questions could rationally be deduced through science, empiricism and reason. From the late 18th century onwards, God would be gradually moved to the margins of both social and political life; intellectually to identify with religious premises would grow to be analogous to anti-intellectualism. The separation of God and the state became the foundation of political thought and social policy. The power of human reason and rationality would be thus deeply relied upon. With God banished from the public sphere, mankind would look to each other and their own "goodness" to mold the world into its better self. So whilst denying God, the world would still search for a better one as long as they would retain their *"freedom"*. The extreme faith in human reason, the desire for world harmony as well as individual freedom would forge a morally relativistic world which was spiritually vacuous and morally shy.

The same human reason that had been exalted in the age of enlightenment when wedded to the excessive freedom and individualism preached, led to moral nihilism. In rejection of God and the basic principles that give value to life the foundations of Western thought gave birth to mini-gods; a vast population of people believing themselves, their reason, their beliefs to be the foundation of not only their lives but the world and not liable to intrusion by dictatorial institutions. At the backdrop of this personal and political drama, the world is wrestling with vast and mounting problems for which we have drafted solutions, yet for which none of the solutions seem to be bearing fruits. The 20th century was the age of social movement; with the fall of great and ancient nations, new ones rose, more or less akin to the previous. Yet in the face of vast and over powering governments people developed an awareness of their inalienable rights and dignity that could not be erased by the titanic states. From the fall of colonial empires to the protests against the evils of war, the 20th century ushered in an age; strengthened by the ideals expressed in the United Nations Declaration of Human Rights; of social protest and the desire to fight the vast and recurring evils in our world. Social consciousness arose in great force, standing side by side with the stubbornness of human desire to destroy, manipulate and conquer. Unlike the ancient times there is no longer a blind obedience to the status quo, and no consciousness that human reason so exalted is fallible.

The denial of a universal objective truth and the embrace of relativism of truth mean that it is ever more difficult to come to a consensus of what ails the world and how to solve those problems. The reliance on reason and empiricism means that the foundation of the world is said to be perceived from what we can see. According to this school of thought, we exist in a one dimensional world. Social sciences also embrace the scientific method of empiricism in attempting to understand society as well as fix its problems. This point of view is the very opposite of God's view; Christianity's view of reality is dualistic. The things of this world are shadow things, reflections of another intangible reality. The Bible begins with God creating the world and then mankind in His own image. God reveals Himself throughout Scripture as Being itself, as Existence and not just the Source of it. According to the account of the fall of man; Adam and Eve's disobedience to God led to a cut off from God and thus from Being. The world that would be forged by their descendants became a fallen world.

Hitherto, I have almost romanticized the relationship of the ancient world with the Divine. Whilst the term atheist was not part of popular vocabulary until much recent history, religion was often used as a means to craft an unjust, unequal and violent world. If anything religion was used both to create and maintain the status quo, much of the alienation to religion that took place during the Enlightenment and the 19th century was due to the gross misuse of power by the church. Religion often meets the ordinary man as the constructed work of feeble and power hungry human minds. Religion is a work of human construction and that has aided in the confinement of God in a box labelled 'rituals' and relegated to the edge of the world He created. Notice the distinction made between God and religion. God made men whilst men made religion, whilst mankind confines God in rituals and laws; God is Essence and Being itself. The Essence-ness of God is opposite to the place He is accorded by the nihilistic and increasingly agnostic world that would rather be left to its 'freedom' and also the church that has embraced the view that the Church and the world are separate. The view of 'the world' taken by the church sadly also encompasses the running of social and political affairs. Of course the precarious history of church relations with the state seems to support this stance; yet it is important to realize that God cannot be held accountable for the erroneous and pernicious actions of those who claimed to work under His directive.

I have stated that the world is now more than ever conscious of the errors of the social, political and economic order. 'We want to change the world', resonates to many people of conscience. Yet in forging the path to that better world, it has already been noted, mankind has come to rely upon their reason and capability. This reliance on human capacity is said to be ungrounded by the bible which locates the issues plaguing the world as grounded in nature i.e. human nature which mankind attained when they fell after Adam's sin.

Christ the Word

In the beginning God spoke the world into existence; by His very breath He brought into being the physical world which we see with our eyes. Yet throughout His walk with man, He has been weaving into the fabric of humanity the design of an inner creation. He has been creating the inner world of His divine Eternal law; the world grounded by His Holiness. Just as the vast universe came into being when God spoke, so the world of God's Holiness was born at the cross when Christ the Word was spoken and the breath of God through Him remade the inner world that had been corrupted by evil. Christ is the Word of God spoken at Calvary marking the start of a new creation, the creative process bringing into reality the design of God. This design is His holiness, echoed in the Lord's Prayer every believer has prayed, *"thy Kingdom come, thy will be done on earth as it is in heaven."* Just as the Word of God made the sun, the moon, the stars and everything on earth and in heaven; so Christ the living Word of God echoes throughout time, past, present and future; and permeates the fabric of the fallen world redesigning and remaking it into the image of God, putting it under the directive of God's eternal law. Christ the Word is placed like a fulcrum in history, the cross is the centre-piece upon which every human being, and every institution must pass through and be redesigned. The Word is heard still and all who answer to His call are made new. He is the spoken Word of God by which the world and all its orders and powers have been remade, ransomed from the world of darkness into the world of light. At the cross we witness a new 'in the beginning', for there; God tears down the curtain of time and places the cross at the start of all time, that all things that are and that have been and that will be are considered *being* only as they are made by Him who is the Word of God. That nothing shall be considered as perfect that is not spoken by the Word and it is only in the Word that the new world is created. So Christ has designed the new world of morals, politics, and economics, social organization; all of which are made according to

His divine law. Such that we say, in the beginning Christ the Word was spoken and in that moment the new world was born. This essay aims to understand the created world of God through Christ, to tear down the illusion that there could be another possible perfect world made outside of God's design through Christ and to show that Christ is the only hope we have for a better world because there is no other Word by which we have been created. There is no greater ideology than the one that states that Christianity has no place in the social, economic, political and even legal organization of human life. The following essay will explore how our essence as a species finds definition within the context of who God says we are. The first section looks at the state of human nature and how having a nature that directs our will affects the world we live in, directs our history and limits our mobility in our attempts to change the world; the second section looks at the evolution of humanity from the nature we are born with into the nature of God and how that evolution is the only hope we have for a better world. The third explores the capacity of our human laws to control and alter human behaviour and looks at how God as justice is the only hope for our world. The fourth section examines the political and social organization of our world and places it against Christ's definition of leadership. The fifth explores the idea of freedom and human rights and it locates the foundations of freedom and human dignity in Scripture. The concluding section looks at how the created Kingdom of God has been made alive in us through the creative Word; Christ and the power of the Holy Spirit.

THE QUESTION OF HUMAN NATURE

I t is only logical that an essay entitled Being should examine first the nature of humans and the world they occupy. The question of what the 'essence' of mankind is has been the subject of philosophical and social thinking for centuries; what is man if anything at all and what does this mean for us is an essential question upon which all other discussions about the being are grounded. There are a plethora of worldviews regarding the issue of human nature yet the one that seems directly contrary to the Christian view is humanism which believes that there is no human nature and humans are burdened to exist first and then create their essence. The Bible however begins with the account of creation; God exists prior to the created things and it is by His design that the created world takes form. In that very garden that God places His first created humans, we witness how the 'inner image' of mankind is corrupted; a corruption that leads God to banish the first created humans and a corruption that taints the rest of mankind. This corruption is human nature and our essence set in stark contrast to the nature of the Word; therefore is without life. This section walks through the avenues of the paradox that is human nature and discovers this nature as a Law in the unseen Universe in control of the seen world and examines what this means for history and our world.

I imagine the very mention of a 'nature' defining man will not sit well in the hearts of most people. The society we live in has taught us to celebrate the freedom and individuality of the person. Centralism whether micro or macro is opposite the dominant narrative in which people have come to think of themselves. We often hear the words, 'you are the master of your own destiny' used to describe and define the human condition and destination. Words like 'fate' and 'destiny' are used as liberally as possible and diluted of the determinism that they denote. *Man is free, man is freedom* stated by Sartre is widely accepted by most people who may not identify themselves as existentialist or may not even know what existentialism is. We have come to identify free will and the ability to make choices with our humanness. According to Sartre, *"there is no universe except the human universe".* The basis of his argument is that, *"...if God does not exist, are we provided with any values or commands which could legitimize our behaviour? Thus we have neither behind us nor before us in a luminous realm of values, any means of justification..."*

What we get from the above thought system is the belief that what we see is what we get; man is responsible for what he is and what he will be and therefore is responsible for the world. Thus according to the humanist stance, man is responsible for his society. Existence precedes essence is the foundation of existentialist thought. The freedom and free will of man is not only ascertained by atheists but by theists as well. We believe that when God created man, He created him a being free to act as he would.

I will begin my argument for human nature at the genesis of time; in the book of Genesis there is reference to a human nature when it is said God made man in His own *image*. After Adam and Eve's sin and subsequent banishment, we witness the debasement of man which is referred to as the 'fall'. Thus in the book of Genesis, we are shown the existence of two different natures; first the nature of God (goodness) which man was first robed in before the fall into the other nature (sin), which became human nature. **Ephesians 2:1-3** state that, *"You used to live in sin, just like the rest of the world, obeying the devil-the commander of the powers of an unseen world. He is the spirit at work in the hearts of those who refuse to obey God. All of us used to live that way, following the passionate desires and inclinations of our sinful nature. By our very nature we were subject to God's anger, just like everyone else."*

From the above verses we come to several conclusions; firstly human nature is revealed as sinful nature which is essentially disobedience to God. Man has come to equate his inability to obey God with freedom or free will. When Adam and Eve disobeyed God they became subject to a different nature, a different way of thinking and acting. The statement, *"by our very nature we were subject to God's anger"*, shows that man does not act by freedom but by *inclination*, an innate wiring within their being that directs them. This wiring is the opposite of God's will. We have come to refer to our disinclination to act according to the will of God as free will, but it is impossible for mankind to act in a spiritual vacuum. *"Mankind never functions independently, autonomously or self generatively. Man is a spiritually dependent creature"*, James A Fowler.

Secondly, the statement*"...obeying the devil-the commander of the powers of an unseen world...the spirit at work in the hearts of those who refuse to obey God"*, shows that man's actions are not the direction of free will but the direction of a spiritual influence. *Essence precedes existence*; defines the condition of man. Thus if man is a spiritually dependent creature, there must always be an inner, prior value system directing his actions. Under whatever power, mankind was always meant to live under a spiritual influence. When mankind fell by disobeying God we lost the right to be God's children meaning we became inclined to disobeying God; there took place another inner remaking of man that severed him from God. Even if one says, but that is not true I choose to do good, I am charitable and kind, I am not subject to human nature, still this would not denounce the argument. That human nature is sinful nature does not mean we are unable to do some good, it means we are naturally inclined to do evil. **Romans 3: 10** states that, *"no one is righteous, not even one."* In the book of Job we witness how human goodness falls short of the standard of God, which is absolute perfection.

Since *essence precedes existence*, man's nature determines what man will be and subsequently what the destiny of the world will be. Since man cannot live in a spiritual vacuum, his essence is defined in an 'unseen world', an intangible world. So the tangible world which we see and feel is the manifestation of an intangible world, far from our senses.

In the book of Isaiah, God says, I will write the law in your heart. This means that by writing His law in the hearts of man so that we might be able to follow it naturally God creates a new nature in man, His nature. Since God's nature acts as a law inside of man, this also follows of sin; it too is a set of innate laws written in the hearts of man. Thus the innate law directs the actions of man. Therefore whatever man is, whatever he does it is the result of another universe outside of the human universe yet controlling it. The 'fallen being' is condemned to live in a void world without the innate knowledge of the One who created it.

The consequence of living in such a world is accentuated when we come to realize that human nature is referred to as a state of slavery. Slavery is a state of being bound, a state the very opposite of the freedom we have come to associate with humanness. The Apostle Paul states that *"I do what I do not want to do and cannot do what I ought to"*, what does this mean for the future of our world? The Hebrew history is a testament of human nature and the consequences of it. Throughout the Old Testament, the Israelites tried and failed dismally to act according to God's laws and standards. Their condition was different from that of the world, which was in a state of abandonment, left to find their own way to a value system. The Jewish law revealed man's sinful nature. Whilst the whole world relied upon their own wisdom to create and forge a better world, the Israelites set against the very opposite of their nature, God's nature, knew how impossible it was to create that world on their own. Hebrew history shows human nature as it is, its 'freedom' is disobedience; its 'wisdom' is foolishness, its 'goodness' falters and it never changes.

The intangible and tangible worlds

In order to understand the importance of human nature; it is imperative to look at the properties of nature. We have established that *essence defines existence.* Adam and Eve corrupted the world when they became subject to sin. The human being who had been given dominion over the world would create institutions and govern the world according to that sinful nature, yet it would be a mistake to assume that it is by his own volition or design that society has taken its shape. *"Fallen man is not able to self-generate anything. He cannot self-generate righteousness or unrighteousness, godliness or ungodliness, saintliness or sinfulness"*, James A Fowler. This means that the created being is created without inner *form;* without *design;* it is a *vessel;* it is nature that is able to give the being its design and pattern the way it will act. Thus there is a prior value system that gives justification for human actions. There is an intangible, unseen universe that directs the tangible and seen universe. The world we live in is a reflection of the laws/value systems of the unseen world that patterns the real world. Meaning if we justify war as a *natural* part of society it means it is a law that controls humans and determines the world the humans build for themselves. This unseen value system as has already been noted, acts as a *power* over creation. Power is directly associated with the taking away of free will. As mankind exists in a world under the dictatorship of sinful nature; he has created institutions devoid of the goodness of God Nature. **Romans 7:21**, *"I have discovered this principle in life that when I want to do what is right, I inevitably do what is wrong. I love God's law with all my heart. But there is another power within me that is at war with my mind. This power makes me slave to sin that is still within me."* The concept of power is also directly associated with *authority;* this authority derives from the fact that nature is a law in the unseen world, a law that humans have no choice but to follow. Thus human nature is derived from an authoritative legal system in the unseen world with the ability to take away the will of people to act, essentially nature defines the basic properties of a being and it is impossible for humans to act in opposition to their nature.

The world of opposites

Human nature has doomed mankind to exist with the consequences of a world devoid of God and it is a recurring struggle to find meaning or values. We exist in a world of opposites; a world of war and peace, injustice and justice, hate and love, chaos and order etc. Everywhere one looks there is an ever resounding call for world peace, for *a better world*. This is the kingdom hanging in the air, the kingdom alive in the hearts of all those who search for light; that better world we look for when we search for justice and peace is God. We live in a binary world, of opposite natures; not tri or quart natures but two natures opposing each other. There is no middle world, forged by the will of man; man has no will with which to create a world or a utopia of choice; the utopia exists within God and it is God's nature we search for when we search for a different world from the one we exist in. We are doomed to oppose the nature we live under, even though we cannot act against it; our conscience still searches for a better *other*. This unending search is revelation of the existence of another nature besides our own; since mankind inherited the curse of Adam, it means *perfect* societies have never existed yet we still advocate for a justice and a peace we have never truly experienced. From where does this desire derive, what gives us the confident hope that the world we wish for is even possible? God has set a desire for Him within His people; even those who search for light without knowing it. Therefore this struggle within the hearts of man and in the world is representative of the struggle between good and evil; against two opposites; two natures and two possible *governments* over the world and over man's heart. We have now deduced the existence of two natures; the nature of God and the nature of Satan. Both natures function as cosmic laws with one as Order, Holiness, Goodness and the other as Chaos, Sinful and Evil. The latter is the Law which governs the human world we live under; its articles direct the moral, legal, social, political and economic worlds we create. The Law of God which we lost at the beginning of time has its own articles too that define the moral, legal, social, political and economic worlds; yet both natures stand in stark contrast to each other because Sin is the negative nature in opposition of God. That it is the negative nature means that it is the Lie and that is why the most refined human minds have always looked for a way out of the systems that govern this world and in essence have always looked for God. Yet what does it mean that the Cosmic Laws act as governments over the world we see? It means that humans have no power to direct their own actions; it means we are born into a world with laws that fashion how we act and how we will treat each other in the micro and macro institutions we build. This is what happened when Adam and Eve disobeyed God; they subjected the whole human race and its future which is also our history to a cosmic legal government that is the very opposite of God and God's journey with mankind throughout time has been to reveal to a people under another nature who He is and at the cross He made complete the recreation of this lost and fallen child. This recreation meant the creation of a being made according to the design of His cosmic Law-Holiness and there is no other way by which mankind can escape the fate of the world he lives except through the recreation by the Word so as to be governed according to God's nature.

What nature as a government means

This opening section has explored the question of human nature and deduced that man does have a nature. This human nature it has been seen controls the actions of man, it acts as a power over man which deprives man of free will. Humans inherited the sinful nature when Adam and Eve disobeyed God. It has also been seen that there exists two natures; God's nature which is good and Satan's nature which is evil. Natures have the capacity to act as laws governing human existence. The nature of God once lost by mankind was made manifest when Christ died on the cross making it possible for humans to live under the spiritual control of good, of God's nature. This is what 'justification by faith' means; because mankind cannot attain good on their own, Christ died and sanctified man making them right with Him. What does this mean for the world? It means that when Christ died He made it possible for the whole world to be governed according to His nature; *holiness*. The world we now exist in is no longer a world under the sole government of sinful nature but there are two *possible natures*. By possible I mean there is the nature we are born with and there is the nature we inherit when we accept Christ; mankind has the choice to choose the good and actually be able to live according to it. This is what it means when it is said, *"you have been given the righteousness of God"*, we have been granted His nature and are able to be His children; able to achieve the better world structured according to His design. The Word still speaks echoing from the cross that exists through all time as the creative Word of God; Christ and as it moves through time it is creating those who will answer to its call; it is remaking those who choose to fall into the will of His design and it is witnessing the birth of a new world under God's eternal Law.

Bible verses from New Living Translation

THE EVOLUTION OF THE RACE

T
he word *evolution* is likely to raise eyebrows and various questions. In an essay aiming precisely to attempt to capture the essence of the world according to God; the reference to evolution, a concept associated with atheism is seemingly paradoxical. However, that we could question that evolution of the species is the purpose of God for His creation is equally eyebrow raising.

From the infancy of the Hebrew nation, God set out to teach the Israelites who to be, and what to be. Yet it has already been shown that man is not self-generative, unable to produce good or evil without a spiritual influence. Since mankind is governed by nature which has a power over them; the transformation advocated by God through the Mosaic Law was impossible. Yet the morphing of His people into an image of perfection was forever the desire of God. Throughout history God was designing mankind through the law and His value system. King Solomon states that God has set eternity in the hearts of man. This eternity is reflected in the development of a historical memory existing in the race. In the ancient Hebrew society although the individual may not have followed every code of law, one felt closeness to God as the child of Abraham, Isaac and Jacob. One could look at society and condemn the actions of unrighteous men not by the discernment of personal wisdom, but by the understanding gathered from the history of his people. The historical memory is seen also in the wider world, the contemporary man may feel himself superior to his ancestors because of the knowledge he has acquired. Yet he may have little understanding that this knowledge has been accumulated over the years, through vast centuries of man building upon the amendment of the errors of their ancestors. This amendment is the outward evolution of the race. The man who says I am far kinder than my ancestors for I would never enslave a man for the colour of his skin is ignorant of the power of the social conscience of the *times* he lives in. In the centuries since slavery, society has come to condemn and find as embarrassing the discrimination of people on the basis of colour and it is condemned ethically and by the law. Yet it would be an illusion for the individual to assume that this instinct derives naturally from his own heart; it is the result of the accumulated racial history and memory.

As society and its values change, the core of the human remains the same, under the control of nature. We have already established that this nature is sinful nature; the opposite of God's nature. God is the grand natural law, an unseen value system with the power to govern the tangible world. It is to be a reflection of this God Nature that man was created and it is to redesign creation according to this value system that Christ died. **Colossians 1: 18** states that *'for God in all his fullness was pleased to live in Christ and through him God reconciled everything to himself. He made everything in heaven and on earth by means of Christ's blood on the cross.'* Thus Jesus became the first of God's *new creation*; a creation under the spiritual control of God Himself. Under the Mosaic Law people were required to offer sacrifices for cleansing of sin; the eternal and everlasting cleansing was made manifest in Christ at the cross. Therefore at the cross all creation is recreated and lifted up from the base nature inherited when Adam and Eve disobeyed God. Thus just as the old creature was subject to evil nature; the new creature; the evolved creation is subject to God's Divine Absolute Law.

The evolution of the creation being designed by God is not an artificial transformation witnessed in the social evolution resulting in the historic memory but the complete *rebirth* that takes place at the core of mankind; it is the death of the spiritual influence of the value system of sin and its replacement with God's nature. This is what is meant when God says, *"I will live in them".* Natural laws that influence the nature of a being are absolute laws that cannot be altered by the desire of man. Thus even though the historical memory alters the mind of man, allowing him to desire the good and not the evil; the good in its absolute perfect state as reflected by God's nature is inconceivable for the man under sin. **Romans 6:18** says, *"now you are free from your slavery to sin and you have become slaves to righteous living"*. This means the Natural laws that influence human nature are absolute; acting as a power over creation. This absoluteness is the perfection of the evolutionary process.

The Universal law is the essence of man that directs the existence of the race. The history of mankind as directed by God would go as –Essence-Existence-Essence. First man existed directed by the nature of sin and at the cross God made it possible for creation to disinherit the nature of sin and to inherit the nature of God. This recreation is the renewal of the human race and therefore the human fate .i.e. his society, the relations and institutions therein. **Isaiah 16:4-5**, *"when oppression and destruction have ended and enemy raiders have disappeared..."* this promise is a reflection of the perfect society envisioned by God, a perfection completed through Christ. In speaking with Nicodemus, Jesus spoke of the necessity of the rebirth of the being; only by this rebirth can the evolution be complete. The concept of rebirth is closely related to reincarnation which can also mean *a new, considerably improved version.* Therefore when the apostle Paul says in **Romans 6:5**, *"since we have been united with him in his death we will also be raised to life as he was"*, it means those who accept Christ become new and improved beings.

Notice we are not talking of a birth but of a re-birth, to be born again from the death experienced under sinful nature; the God Nature is life. Mankind enters the world in the possession of an opposite nature; a negative nature; meaning *not the original.* God created mankind to be His heritage to be a reflection of His Essence (goodness). When mankind lost that they began to exist in a negative world pressing towards the positive. However *"mankind did not need a new system of rehabilitation or reformation to deal with their sinful ways and the consequences of death. Additional rules and regulations to try to effect behavioural modification will not suffice"* - James A Fowler.

In essence only the regeneration of mankind to the image of God can complete the evolution of the race. *"By the initiative of His grace through His Son Jesus Christ, God has accomplished everything necessary to restore mankind to the function intent for which He created him. That intent was that the life and character of God might be present within the man, allowing for the expression of such in man's behaviour unto the glory of God"* -James A Fowler.

> *"Christ as the Image of the Perfect World*
> There can be only one permanent revolution
> A moral one: the regeneration of the inner man...
> Yet in our world everybody thinks of changing humanity
> And nobody thinks of changing himself."
> *Leo Tolstoy 1900*

The word *revolution* incites images of protest or violent mass movements that are not synonymous with Christian teachings yet how else can we define Christ's teachings other than *revolutionary*. By definition a revolution is the removal or replacement of a government. We already know that human nature exercises influence over people — it is a government over the hearts of people. In the process of inner evolution, God replaces the government of sin with the government of His holiness. This inner revolution is the *only* change that can permanently alter the world into a perfect world; a God influenced world.

We live in a social movement society, movements that started with the European revolutions of the 18th Century and accentuated in the last Century. In realizing the imperfections of our societies and our governments we have sought to build utopias, to build better worlds either through violent or non-violent means. We have set up titanic institutions such as the United Nations, we have set up awards to honour those who fight for a better world, we spend a lot of money in the intellectual improvement of the being yet this is the artificial evolution of the being; incapable of permanently changing the human and his condition. Only the inner reformation of the being is the permanent evolution. The human method of changing the world begins with the need to change the external world. Everywhere we set out to change a social condition by toppling leaders, by changing policies or by marching in the streets for our voices to be heard little understanding that the outer world is the creation of the inner man; the sinful man. Pro-agency theorists are of the view that the individual is the centre of society; creating great institutions by their agency even though those institutions become so big that they overshadow and control the individuals who make them. Yet the fact remains that social institutions are designed by humans, humans under the control of sinful nature. How then can the advocates for a better world get rid of these evils when they are fighting against human nature and essentially fighting against that which lives in them as well? This we have already noted is impossible mankind cannot fight his essences because it is a law written in nature itself.

In order to change the world, man must change himself first. Be transformed by the renewal of your mind, the word says. Yet the renewal of the mind is not the artificial renovation gained through worldly education but the transformation of the inner being by Christ Jesus. Jesus is the image of the perfect, new creation; the first born of God's new creation. He is the author of the moral reformation that must take place in all creation. Love is the foundation of Christian thinking. This love; agape love; taught by Jesus was revolting against the basic instincts of man. Man's instincts tell him to retaliate in the face of aggression; self-preservation is a primal human instinct. Yet Jesus teaches us to turn the other cheek in the face of violence; He teaches us to not resist evil. He teaches us to go the extra mile in the face of repression.

To a people so used to showing their acts of generosity for the world to see, Jesus taught a humility that is self-denying to the human ego. Set in the backdrop of the extravagance of the hypocritical

Pharisees; Jesus set out to challenge both the actions of the sect and the nature of man. It is hardly natural for people to give and have no outward recognition of their generosity. Acts of kindness, He taught must be done in private; in fact He said, *"what your right hand has done let not your left know."* This is a call for genuine kindness; unmotivated by the need for praise.

We know our instincts tell us to hate those who hate us and to fight against our oppressors; yet in revolt Jesus teaches us to love those who hate us and pray for those who oppress us. Imagine the person who loathes you the most; the person who will miss no chance to harm or humiliate you. That is the person Jesus teaches us to love; He too displayed that love when He asked God for the deliverance of His enemies upon His crucifixion. To Him this is true religion and He gives this not as an option; the unconditional blind love is the sign of His nature. Of His followers He commands them to 'love your neighbours as you love yourselves.' Imagine what kind of love this is, a love that does to others as one would expect to be done to them. This He says is the teaching of the prophets, for where would we find slavery, war, oppression, repression, racism, sexism, hunger or poverty if such love was the law of the world. Yet this love is available to those who believe in Him and who accept His nature into their hearts. Jesus showed the perfection of God in man, as hope that we too can achieve such perfection through Him.

He gives His commands for all to follow. It is not a call for a mass movement but for an inner movement, a replication of His image and His deeds through works. It is this denial of violence, the rejection of outer strength for inner strength, the rejection of self-centeredness and embrace of universal brotherhood and sisterhood, the rejection of enmity and embrace of meekness that is the path to a better world. It is mankind's natural inclinations that make him susceptible to discrimination, it is our love for glory that has led to the oppression of vast populations and races of people, it is our inability to put ourselves in others' shoes; our inability to do to others as we would have them do to us that makes racism and other forms of oppression possible. It is our inability to resist evil, to give in to anger and our principle of 'an eye for an eye', that makes wars possible. The recurring evils of the world that we wish so vehemently to end are a result not of the giant states or institutions, but of man whose conscience does not condemn him of these things. As Jesus revolts against these natural inclinations and teaches and commands us to follow another way; in that there is hope for change. For men of sinful nature in consensus perpetrate the great evils of the world and these evils can only be combated by a moral revolution within the heart of every man.

The Kingdom of God in us

This renovation of the mind of man is the hope for the world. It is a hope that is made complete through the Spirit of God, the third person of the Trinity. Jesus said of Him; *"When the Spirit of truth comes He will guide you into all truth."* The Holy Spirit is God manifest in the hearts of those who believe, He is God residing in the earthly vessels; He is the Nature of God made manifest and alive within the believers; His is the baptism that makes manifest the rebirth and the reformation of the inner being. Just like we once were slaves to the spirit of Satan bearing his fruits; we become captive to the Holy Spirit bearing fruits of God. The third Person of the Holy Trinity is the completion of the evolution; He makes manifest the kingdom of God within man; *He is the Kingdom of God alive in believers.* He makes complete the moral revolution and it is through His works that God's kingdom is made alive in us. In essence He is the Law of God active in the people who had lost that divine Law and He is the government of God within the regenerated being. The Spirit of God is the spiritual influence of God in mankind, the new God Nature making it possible for humans to function in accordance to the will of God, thus making powerless the authority of sinful nature and making manifest another authority and power in us. It is only through the Spirit of God that the recreation process is made complete for we are vessels filled with Him and He is God Himself at work in His creation transforming them into His evolved and perfect creatures. If it seems too hard to believe it is because we have relied unjustly upon our own efforts yet the only process that can change mankind is the process of inner reformation .i.e. for the active power of God's Law to become alive in mankind. As the Word travels through the walls of time, it lives within those it meets and those who stop for it, they are coloured by His design and made perfect in order to exhibit His perfection to the world. It is not revolution nor war, not education nor new theories that will change the world but only the evolution of the race created by the Word that can perfect the world.

LAW AND JUSTICE

T

he writing of this section coincides with a court case in our country against prominent officials being accused of corruption. As I watched the proceedings I could not help but be fascinated by the legal system's method for a quest for *justice* at the same time I could see the hope of those who watched; the hope in the system and the authority figures; hope that they would bring justice. There existed a sort of dichotomy in the minds of people; the divide between the *guilty* and the *innocent*. As the prosecution presented their argument the onlookers laughed almost in condemnation of the accused, pronouncing judgment of guilt. This is the system that has been used throughout history as a means of social control, yet the question is how effective is the legal system in bringing about the justice we so vehemently search for. Is the legal system able to truly alter human behaviour and bring about a state of order?

According to Andrei Marmor (2011), the law is by and large a system of norms. Law's essential character is *prescriptive:* it purports to *guide action, alter* modes of behaviour, *and constrain* the practical *deliberations* of its subjects. The English dictionary defines law as one of the two metaphysical forces of the world in some fantasy settings as opposed to *chaos.* Thus the need for law in society presupposes the existence of a state of chaos, an innate disorder that needs to be made right. The prescriptive nature of law presupposes a nature that is wayward, this too is supported by the fact that law aims not only to guide human behaviour but to alter it. The fact that law is both *normative* and it aims to make an *alteration* means that the social reality which makes law necessary is not moral therefore must be changed to something better. Furthermore the law aims to constrain or to change by force the deliberations and intentional actions of its subjects. It aims to overpower the nature of man. *"Legal positivism can concede that the law is necessarily good, if it is true that human nature, or the nature of human society is such that makes it necessary to have law"*, Marmor (2011).

Human nature which has already been noted as sinful is indeed in need of change, but can this change be effected by the instrument of law. Law exists to solve moral and political problems existing in society, it is designed to act as a bridge from one way of living to another and the ends of that are morality and justice by means of force. Thus law is both normative and forceful. *"The main function of most legal norms is to actually guide the conduct of law's subjects. Thus law is not simply theoretical but its validity must be seen in the ability of people to abide by it. The idea of legal validity as Kelsen admits, is closely tied to this reality of a social practice, a legal system exists, as it were, only as a social reality-a reality that consists in the fact that people actually follow certain norms"*, (Marmor 2011). Yet as a system of rules and regulations meant to provide the direction for human behavior, can law alter the actions of its subjects; in essence can law as an instrument change human nature? Law relies not only on its prescriptive nature but, according to Marmor, *"law's enforcing mechanism, its ability to compel behaviour by use of force, is what makes the law a unique instrument of social control."* Laws purport to change behaviour through punishment for wrong doing or the threat of it to ensure peaceful co-existence of people. This is the system that humanity has relied upon for justice, peace and morality.

Human nature versus Human law

We have stated that human nature makes it necessary for there to be an instrument of control in place. By definition nature means *conformity to that which is natural, as distinguished from that which is artificial, or forced.* Nature is what one will do on their own, distinct from what might be expected thus human law is artificial; it cannot compel its subjects to act according to its dictates because they are already subject to another superior legal system which is written in nature. The normative nature of law cannot alter human inclination to act in certain ways; it can direct human conscience but it cannot effectively act as an instrument of change and rehabilitation for it offers an artificial change that does not deal with the innate chaos within man and subsequently his society.

"If E is an end we necessarily have and L is a necessary instrument to achieve E, then L is necessarily good..." (Marmor 2011). We have ascertained that morality, justice and social control are the ends of law. That is not to say all law is just or fair, history has sufficient evidence against this, but almost every legal system when being drafted is done so under the perception that it will bring forth the moral and just standards of that society. If this justice, morality and order are the ends we want, then we must examine how the law as an instrument purports to attain these. We have seen that the law is *prescriptive*; it aims to act as a diagnosis for what ails society .i.e. human nature. Since the law is artificial attempting to alter the natural actions of man through rules and regulations, we must give it the position of a secondary law; the primary and main law being the law of nature. Thus when a law says 'do not steal', it is first of all recognizing the natural inclinations of humans to steal and then setting up a rule in order to ensure that people do not steal. Now if a person is caught stealing and tried under the law; it does not mean that the law has taken away the natural deliberation of that individual, they may go back to stealing again. The law then is only an artificial instrument that aims to maintain order through a system of rules.

At the same time almost every legal system is grounded by force, rules alone without the threat of punishment are insufficient. The police, lawyers, judges, prisons and correctional services are instruments of force within the legal system such that when the law says, 'do not steal or else...' it refers to how these instruments of law will have to respond in the event that there has been a theft. It is the fear of consequences that is relied upon to alter human behaviour and to control society. If the force of punishment was sufficient to alter societal behaviour then no crimes would be committed, it's safe to say that the law was put in place as the *other* of the innate chaos existing within people and society. Yet human law is not the natural opposite of this chaos, the Law of Order is. All legal systems will state that they are standing up for truth, justice, fairness and what is good yet all of these in their pure form are found in the metaphysical opposite of chaos; God. Thus it is the Nature of God, the law of God that is the natural opposite of the chaos, human laws attempt to fight albeit clouded by the deficiencies of our limited minds and standards. Before giving a conclusive verdict it is imperative to turn to the idea of justice and examine how the law aims to achieve this.

Justice

The earliest memory I have of the idea of justice comes from childhood games, it is there that I was introduced to the idea of fairness, to the need for rules in order to keep the peace and I learnt of punishment when rules were broken. As I grew older and the concept of justice was refined; it is the image of the blindfolded woman holding the scales that appears; justice is impartial; justice is fair and justice is blind we are told. Justice is defined as a state of being *just* and *fair* and also as *judgment* and *punishment* of a party that has wronged another. Thus the law is closely tied to justice. It is the use of force and punishment that is trusted to alter human behaviour; to get rid of wrong or evil; to bring justice. The word *just* means *correct, morally right, upright, and righteous. Righteous* in turn means free from sin or guilt or *sanctimonious* which means *perfect or flawless.* Thus the law aims to bring to justice the wrongdoer and to give justice to the wronged, it aims to justify, to find one morally right, perfect and flawless and to condemn another of guilt. That is our definition of justice.

'Understanding the theory of original sin will free us from thinking about evil and injustice in the world in terms of an

us(good) versus them(bad) dichotomy. Evil and injustice are not merely external, the problem of evil is not simply or purely a cosmic thing; it is also a problem about me. Therefore the intersection of faith and justice on issues of religious persecution, racism, inequality, exploitation, discrimination and the neglect of vulnerable populations starts with us. Knowing that all mankind are by nature in a state of total ruin, both with respect to the moral evil of which they are subjects, and the afflictive evil to which they are exposed, the one as the consequence and the punishment of the other is key to guiding our steps towards making the world a better place. We are all sinners and complicit in the evil that plagues our world and our condition necessitates God's rescue plan.' (Wilson 2016)

Therefore since we are all under the control of sinful nature and since the law through its rules, guidance and force cannot alter our behaviour, it cannot *justify* anyone. It can neither condemn the guilty since we are all guilty; it can declare no one *free from sin or guilt*. The only way by which we are made sanctimonious is through the salvation power of Christ. True justice which is to make just and perfect is not achievable through the rehabilitation system which is unable to renew the being to a state of flawlessness. The law cannot condemn because the problem it aims to deal with is not a problem of deviance, it is a problem of a nature alive and active in all humans.

'The first point that struck me when I understood the commandment, 'Do not resist evil,' in its true meaning, was that human courts were not only contrary to this commandment, but in direct opposition to the whole doctrine of Christ, and that therefore He must certainly have forbidden them. Christ says. 'Do not resist evil.' The sole object of courts of law is to. Christ says, 'Make no distinction between the just and

the unjust.' Courts of law do nothing else. Christ says, 'Forgive all. Forgive not once, not seven times, but forgive without end.' 'Love your enemies.' 'Do good to those who hate you.'...In the case of the adulteress He (Jesus) positively rejects human justice and proves that, on account of each man's own sinful nature, he has no right to judge another...According to the gospels of Matthew and Luke, the texts, 'Do not judge; do not condemn,' are preceded by the words, 'Do not resist evil, suffer evil, do good to all.' In the gospel according to Matthew the words of the Hebrew criminal law are repeated, 'An eye for an eye, a tooth for a tooth.' And after citing the criminal law, Christ says, 'But you are not to act thus; do not resist evil.' Then He goes on to say, 'Do not judge.' So Christ's words refer precisely to our human criminal law, and by the words, 'Do not judge.' He clearly rejects it... In chapter 4, verses 11 and 12, the disciple James says, 'Do not speak evil of one another, brethren. He who speaks evil of his brother, and judges his brother, speaks evil of the law, and judges the law; but if you judge the law, you are not a doer of the law, but a judge. There is one lawgiver, who is able to save...' 'A judge,' Christ says, 'is he who can save.' (Leo Tolstoy 1886).

Therefore if only the one who can save can judge and if only God can save; then we must look to the justice of God for answers on justice in the world. It has been stated that, *"if E is an end we necessarily have and L is a necessary instrument to achieve E then L is necessarily good,"* (Marmor 2011). We know that the law is unable to eradicate human evil, which is the end we must have therefore human justice falls short. The justice of God declares innocent the guilty by eradicating the power of sin, of the inner chaos within man through redemption. As Christians we must look at the doctrine of redemption for answers to the problems that plague the world; from inequality, bondage, racism, discrimination to war; we find justice in God's ability to restore the fallen world to His Nature; that is Justice. This is the only way to solve the moral and political problems of the world. True justice occurs when we have rendered the law obsolete, that is; when we have overcome the state of inner and outer chaos we live under and achieved its opposite; Order. This is achievable when the law is made alive and active in us in the same way chaos was. Only by the evolution of the being into the metaphysical opposite of chaos; a transformation into an innate obedience of that which could not be coerced can true justice be said to be achieved. The method by which God achieves this is redemption, through salvation.

Through salvation God makes it possible for the blemish and power of sin to be wiped out; that means he destroyed the active power of sin; the very nature that made human law possible - the same nature that created the moral and political problems for which we made laws to begin with. God made it possible for Order, the moral, social and political order we aim to create through the law; to be active by nature within humans. So when it is said that God made it possible for humans to live without the directives of the law it does not mean God substitutes law for a state of disorder; it simply means that since we are made sanctimonious and perfect through salvation, the state of order we aim to achieve through the artificial law is made alive in us. Jesus said, *"heaven and earth will pass away but not an article of the law of Moses will pass away"*, thus when He says that He came to fulfil the law He simply means He came to make it possible for all people who are saved through Him and by Him to follow the directives of God's righteousness by nature. Thus it is through the Word of God, Christ, that the Law of God is birthed within the world of man making a transference of all people who respond to His calling and design their societies according to His directive, from the law of chaos to the divine, righteous Law of God that obliterates the hatred, injustice, discrimination and evil in the world.

POLITICS AND SOCIAL ORGANIZATION

M

ichel Foucault stated that *there are forms of oppression and domination which become invisible-the new normal.* We are born in a world with existing patterns, a world of rules, regulations, behaviours, practices and structures that we are expected to follow without question and we believe them to be normal. That is how power and domination are exercised in their highest form, within *common sense*. In Roth's *Divergent* the characters live in a society of factions that expects the normal citizens to be one dimensional, those displaying multiple traits are regarded as abnormal. That is how society works, it is a constructed world with norms we do not question; our own one dimensional world that we cannot question because it is the only reality there ever was. Yet if anything the preceding segments have challenged us to hope, to believe in the existence of another **normal** better than the one we have now.

We live in well patterned societies that no matter how apparently diverse they are, the underlying rules that guide them are the same. For example, almost all societies have groups, these groups appear to have been drawn in permanent ink in the beginning of time, we don't question why they are there and we cannot imagine them not being there. We have the rich and the poor and everything else in between; we have the powerful and the powerless; those who direct the actions of others and those who are directed. There are the wars we fight without quite questioning their logic or morality - we are told they are honourable. There are expensive clothes and gadgets we buy because that's what everyone else is doing without questioning how we are taking part in consumerism and how as a symptom of the times we live in it affects the poor among us. We are all of us in a labyrinth just following the path with little asking if it is the right way and if maybe there could be another way, another normal. This section explores our political, social and economic normal and places it besides the Christian ideal of political, social and economic perfections, in essence; it questions our normal and walks us through the other better normal.

The word politics invokes images of power, honour, status, nobility and the various tactics used to get the game going. Almost all political theories presuppose the idea of power; it is power that is first given to an individual or individuals and then the theory goes on to explain what legitimizes that power and how it will be used and to what extent. Whether we are speaking of a monarchy, autocratic or even democratic government; leaders are held to be above the 'mob', either through the 'vote' of the people or through 'divine right'. There are a few words that are associated with politics.

Firstly there is *power* which means the ability to coerce, influence or control. Coercion in turn is physical or moral force to compel a person to do something or to abstain from doing something thereby depriving that person the ability to exercise free will:

♣ To *Rule* means to be in charge of or make decisions for and to reign over.

♣ *Government* is a group of people who hold a monopoly on the legitimate use of force in a given territory.

From the above definitions we can deduce certain things; firstly governments rely on coercion or ideology to take away the will of the people. In fact according to Hobbes the main rationale of political sovereignty in terms of monopolizing the use of force is in order to pacify society and ensure peaceful co-existence of individuals. So the argument is that people's nature requires force in order to be put in check or else there would be chaos and brutality everywhere. In other words the brutality, coercion and pacification of individuals by government; in short the overt and ideological violence is necessary for peace. There is no need to point out the paradox. Secondly all governments presume, assert and exercise superiority and authority over people and their affairs. They see it as their right to be above and superior to people. In fact under the control of governments people are first of all placed under governments and under their shadows they are pacified by physical and ideological force and this pacification brings order and peace; it is said.

Throughout history humans have tried and tested various forms of governments and the above notions have almost always accompanied these governments. We know of great empires; we know of the conquests of the Roman Empire, the autocratic monarchies of Europe, the colonial empires of Britain, France, Spain and other European countries and also of the dictatorships that replaced them. We have tried the 'egalitarian' communism which ended up as brutal as all others and whilst Americans were oppressing blacks within their own realm and Britain and other colonialists were performing brutal cruelties in colonies, their leaders thought of democracy which was held to be the hope of a utopia. We have tried and tested democracy and we have seen how the exclusion, bribery, election violence and corruption involved with it classes it among the other forms of governments.

The problem with our idea of governance is its reliance on violence to keep order and also the top-down structure of governments. We hear of HIS or Her Royal Highness, HIS or HER Excellency the president. Already by their titles leaders assert their supposed superiority over the people whose interests they are supposed to serve. They attain great wealth and honour as the 'privilege' of birth or of the work they have not yet done. They attain the allegiance of the armies and the authority figures; the courts of law and the police and with honour, wealth and power they are expected to act in the interest of the people; can a lion act in the interest of sheep?

Yet as we have already stated humans are under the control of a nature, a negative nature and the laws of this nature reflect in the institutions we build, politics included of course. This means that the ethical standing of people directly influences how governments rule over us. No matter how theoretically sound and just our political theories are, unethical people will always corrupt them. So we are dealing with the problem of nature; the nature of our political governance which has reverberated throughout history and darkened it.

We have said that just leadership has failed because human leaders rely on force, extreme power and wealth as well as superiority over people. Jesus turns the idea of leadership on its head. We live in a dichotomous world of opposite natures, so when I say Jesus turned the idea of leadership on in its head I essentially mean he defined and exercised leadership as it is in the nature of God. When the Israelites asked for a king after their dissatisfaction with Samuel and God as their leaders this is God's warning to them.

This is how a king will reign over you. The king will draft your sons and assign them to his chariots and charioteers, making them run before his chariots. Some will be generals and captains in his army, some will be forced to plough in his fields and harvest his crops and some will make his weapons and chariot equipment. The king will take your daughters from you and force them to cook and bake and make perfumes for him. He will take away the best of your fields and vineyards and olive groves and give them to his own officials. He will take a tenth of your grain and your grape harvest and distribute it among his officers and attendants. He will take your male and female slaves and demand the finest of your cattle and donkeys for his own use. He will demand a tenth of your flocks and you will be his slaves.

Samuel 8: 10-17

God denies the method by which leaders would rule over the people, what we see here is a rejection of the superiority of leaders even in the most basic form. To us it is the norm for leaders to have escorts and convoys, their station allows it we reason; yet God clearly states it is unjust. Who can deny that leaders need state or palace servants to wait on them, cook for them and ensure they live the most labour-free and luxurious life. Yet again God classes it with all the other injustices of leaders. We have often heard of state property or property belonging to the crown or monarchy; in most cases we do not question this; we say it comes with the job. Most crown and government properties distributed among members of royal families and state officials are worth billions. We praise this as glamorous yet God judges it as unjust. We do not question that the state demands money from citizens as tax yet here it is clearly refuted. All the above mentioned things are part of the structure and daily running of a government; the leaders are above us, we don't question this, they are of royal blood or elected or qualified so they do have a right to be above us 'common' people, we say. Yet to God the opposite is true, the leader is the servant of the people and not the other way round. The lion must serve the sheep.

After washing their feet, he put on his robe again and sat down and asked, 'Do you understand what I was doing? You call me 'Teacher' and 'Lord' and you are right that's what I am. And since I your Lord and Teacher have washed your feet, you ought to wash each other's feet. I have given you an example to follow. Do as I have done to you. I tell you the truth, slaves are not greater that their master. Nor is the messenger more important than the one who sends the message... **John 13:12**

But Jesus called them together and said, 'You know that the rulers in this world lord it over their people and officials flaunt their authority over those under them. But among you it will be different. Whoever wants to be a leader among you must be your servant, and whoever wants to be the first among you must become your slave. For the Son of Man came not to be served but to serve others and to give his life as a ransom for many."

Matthew 20:25-28

In the gospel of Luke Jesus says those who wish to be the greatest must occupy the lowest rank. This is what leadership is to Jesus:-service. Yet before we begin to dismiss it as an abstract concept let us look at the ways Jesus himself demonstrated it. He; God Himself, the Creator and Lord of all the Universe incarnated as the son of a lowly carpenter and was born in a manger. He could have been born as an earthly royal prince but instead He chose humility. At the last supper He washed His disciples' feet, which was a very lowly task done by servants. On His entry in Jerusalem He rode on a donkey instead of a magnificent horse fit for the King of all worlds. He ascended His throne crowned with a crown of thorns and briars as well as a purple robe of mockery. His title was written upon planks on the cross that symbolized the burdens of His people. He is the true Servant King and if He the King of kings so humbly carried himself, He expects the same of every leader whether political or religious.

The term 'lord it over' means to behave as if one is in control of, to make a display of having an advantage over or superiority to. It also means higher in rank. Yet this is the very definition of leaders' positions in our society; their leadership entitles them to a higher position. Jesus expects and acts the very opposite, He who is the greatest becomes the least, the master becomes the servant and the slave. We might say yes but He was Jesus of course He could do it; but He gave it as a command not to heavenly beings but to earthly people. Our governments have failed us and will continue to do so as long as the leaders continue to flaunt their authority. Here I imagine images of anarchy arising to your mind. Anarchy is the belief that proposes the absence and abolition of hierarchy and authority in most forms. Hierarchy by definition is a social, religious, economic or political system in which people are ranked, with some superior to others based on their status, authority or some other trait. Whilst Jesus does not abolish hierarchy or authority he states that those who occupy the positions of authority must act as though they are the lowest - this on its own does away with the overt and repressive hierarchal systems of the world. In the true Christian sense though; this state cannot be brought about by violent revolution which breeds chaos but on its own through the evolution of the inner beings.

Leo Tolstoy, The kingdom of God is Within You (1894) Chapter X

> *Christianity in its true sense puts an end to government. So it was understood at its very commencement; it was for that cause that Christ was crucified. So it has always been understood by people who were not under the necessity of justifying a Christian government. Only from the time that the heads of government assumed an external and nominal Christianity, men began to invent all the impossible, cunningly devised theories by means of which Christianity can be reconciled with government. But no honest and serious-minded man of our day can help seeing the incompatibility of true Christianity-the doctrine of meekness, forgiveness of injuries, and love-with government, with its pomp, acts of violence, executions and wars. The profession of true Christianity not only excludes the possibility of recognizing government, but even destroys its very foundations.*

The Christian doctrine is incompatible with government as it stands because it professes a whole different kingdom from that which we live under. In the book of Daniel we are told of King Nebuchadnezzar's dream of a statue representing all the kingdoms that would reign over the earth; this statue would be crushed by a rock cut off from a mountain. This rock is said to symbolize that promised kingdom of God that will reign forever. This is the kingdom bought by blood and suffering whose king wears a crown of thorns and a robe coloured royal by His blood. It is the kingdom where the highest is also the lowest.

The form of leadership which was professed and practiced by Jesus renounces all superiority and power in the coercive sense we know it. This is servant leadership. Now let us look closely at the attributes of servants, slaves and lowest ranked people. Anyone who has ever read *Twelve years a slave the autobiography of Solomon Northup* can get the picture of what we mean when we say a slave. A typical day for a slave involved waking up very early before dawn, working nonstop under scotching heat or brutal cold with only about a ten minute break in between for food. Stopping during work was not allowed and it was followed by lashes from the overseer. The slave had no rights; he was the lowest of the low. The poor whites found comfort in their position in the fact that they were at least higher than the slaves. If slaves even tried to run away they were followed and tracked down by dogs which were allowed to kill or terribly wound them. Usually the slaves were made to work until the last light; that is near or after midnight. The sole existence of the slave revolved around working for the master. Yet Jesus says of those who wish to be leaders they must be the slaves of the led, the lowest ranked. And Jesus did not mean this as an abstract concept; an ideal; He meant it literally. This is the rock from the mountain the only sustainable political theory that must replace monarchy, autocracy, oligarchy, dictatorship and democracy; the Servant-Leadership.

Non-violence and an end to war

It has been stated that governments justify their very existence upon the premise that without force order and justice cannot prevail. Thus the state requires the army to protect it; the legal system rests upon the force of the police and imprisonment. We exist in a society of confinement, both physically and ideologically. And that confinement resulting in pacification is intended for us to accept as common sense the idea that force begets peace. There could be no greater ideology than that. An eye for an eye is the ideology of the state.

Leo Tolstoy, Christianity and Patriotism (1895) as translated in The Novels and Other Works of Lyof N. Tolstoi, Vol. 20

In all history there is no war which was not hatched by the governments, the governments alone, independent of the interests of the people, to whom war is always pernicious even when successful.

The government assures the people that they are in danger from the invasion of another nation, or from foes in their midst, and that the only way to escape this danger is by the slavish obedience of the people to their government. This fact is seen most prominently during revolutions and dictatorships, but it exists always and everywhere that the power of the government exists. Every government explains its existence and justifies its deeds of violence, by the argument that if it did not exist the condition of things would be very much worse. After assuring the people of its danger the government subordinates it to control and when in this condition compels it to attack some other nation. And thus the assurance of the government is corroborated in the eyes of the people, as to the danger of attack from other nations.

Governments are inherently violent and there is no other body responsible for more violence than the government as it stands with its foundation upon force. The Just war theory would have you believe there are cases where war is indeed necessary and in our nature which would rather preserve the self than forgive the enemy we accept that if there is a threat from within or without we must indeed retaliate by force. The just war theory states that war must have a just cause such as self-defence, the protection of the innocent from aggression or the corrective punishment for past wrongs. This is in stark contrast to the Christian doctrine which preaches meekness, pacifism and forgiveness. **Romans 12:21** states that *"Do not be overcome by evil but overcome evil by good"*. At the Sermon on the Mount Jesus tells His followers that *"you have heard the law that says the punishment must match the injury.*

An eye for an eye and a tooth for a tooth, but I say do not resist an evil person. If someone slaps you on the right cheek, offer the other cheek also," **(Matthew 5:38-39).** Thus the very idea that war can be justified by the argument of self-defence is false. Violence does not bring an end to violence; it can only violate the rights of people and bring suffering, death and destruction. Only peace can bring about peace. The just war theory also states that the decision to go to war must be made by the right authorities. It also states that the intention for war must be just and not for material gain. Yet how many wars have been fought by the 'authorities' for oil, land that did not belong to them, influence in regions of free peoples? That there could be an 'authority' with the right to declare the deaths of thousands of innocent people, to destroy the peaceful existence of races and displace them from their homes is a great ideology. There is no nobility in murder; worse still in mass murder and that is what war is; the mass murder of people. There is no authority over the lives of people except God Himself and the same God declared that the peacemakers will inherit the kingdom of heaven. It is paradoxical that most wars in Europe during the last few centuries have been on religious grounds. There is no compatibility between a gospel that proclaims meekness and love for our enemies and the religious wars monarchies waged against their people and other lands. The doctrine of just war seems to argue that if we reflect enough darkness upon the world there will be light. The just war theory also states that the *good* done in war must outweigh the evil. Yet even the loss of a single life in war does not justify it, what possible good could be justified by the deaths of the people in past wars, wars that are happening now and those that are yet to happen? War is the ideology of the powerful that are untouched by it, those who are not afraid to sacrifice the masses for power.

Jesus is called the King of Justice and the King of Peace; it is righteousness that is the foundation of His kingdom. In the book of Revelations the Apostle John sees a rider on a white horse whose title is the Word of God. Thus Jesus did not wage the war against evil by slaughter He won it through the saving power of His Word. It is the sacrifice of Christ, the salvation and righteousness it brings that ushers Justice and Peace and not the evil of war. Pope Francis stated that, *"war is suicide of humankind. War must be rejected. Violence must be rejected."* Whilst our governments justify themselves by violence, God states in the book of Isaiah, *"the Lord will mediate between nations and will settle international disputes. They will hammer their swords into ploughshares and their spears into pruning hooks. Nation will no longer fight against nation, nor train for war anymore"*, (Isaiah 2:4). In another passage He says, *"the boots of the warrior and the uniforms blood-stained by war will all be burnt. They will be fuel for the fire. For a child is born to us, a son is given to us. The government will rest on his shoulders"*, (Isaiah 9:5-6). Who then can deny that nonviolence is one of the key cornerstones of Christian beliefs? Can a government that professes itself to be Christian base its power on violence against its own people and others? And can a Christian become a soldier and call murder for the state honourable?

The state and Christianity are conflicting ideals that do not and cannot meet. It is to put an end to all violence and to bring peace that Christ was crucified, He carried the burden of the government on His shoulder, and He is the Prince of Peace. Upon the cross He set aside His sufferings and asked God to forgive the very people who had crucified Him, yet we say self-defence justifies war when God did not defend Himself against those weaker than Him. Yet through pacifism He achieved good for eternity and all generations.

The Community Economy

The 20th Century was coloured by the struggle between communism and capitalism. Communist governments arose proclaiming the ideology of a common economy for all people, a classless society as proclaimed and envisioned by Karl Marx. But the vision of Marx did not quite work out as communist governments became authoritarian. Today still most governments which proclaim to be communist are so in theory only; such that the idea of a communist society has been altogether abandoned as idealistic. One of the main reasons why communism failed is because these governments following the directive of Marx rose through violent revolutions. Marxism after all is a conflict theory. To Marx, only the revolution of the proletariat can bring about the communist society. And as with all revolutions there must always emerge two main classes, the vanquished and the victors. Yet without an egalitarian and moral political reality, communism is doomed to fail, and not just as a political theory but as an ethical one too.

We have discussed how the condition of human nature affects the societies that people build and no matter how egalitarian a theory may be our corrupted and defective nature will always corrupt it. The question of the ethical condition of the being is the first thing to consider when speaking of political, social and economic issues. It is the ethical condition that determines our world. The society we live in is both capitalist and consumerist. The effect is the increasing gap between the rich and the poor both at national and global levels. Whilst I will not get into detail with this, I will state that the world continues to look for solutions to end global poverty whilst still clinging to capitalism and consumerism; that is oxymoronic. Socialism is truly the only solution to global poverty, yet it is directly opposed to the interests of the powerful.

Our ethical theory has stated that we are dealing with an issue of human nature and not simply human deeds, human nature affects world systems. We have tried socialism and it has failed because at its core human nature does not change unless altered into the nature of God through salvation. Socialism itself has religious roots as opposed to Marx's materialism. Upon handing down the Jewish law God instructed, *"Plant and harvest your crops for six years but let the land be renewed and lie uncultivated during the seventh year. Then let the poor among you harvest whatever grows on its own. Leave the rest for the wild animals to eat. The same applies to your vine yards and olive groves",* (Exodus 23:10-11). The same message is echoed by John the Baptist when he urged people to give to the needy, *"whoever has two coats must share with anyone who has none and whoever has food must do likewise",* (Luke 3:11). Jesus told the rich young ruler that if he wanted to follow he should have to give up his possessions and give them to the poor. We may dismiss this saying Jesus did not mean we should change the economic system only that the rich should relieve the burden of the poor, however a look at how the early church lived proves otherwise.

All the believers devoted themselves to the apostles' teachings and to fellowship, and to sharing in meals (including the Lord's Supper) and to prayer. A deep sense of awe came over them all, and the apostles performed many miraculous signs and wonders. And all the believers met together in one place and shared everything they had. They sold their property and possessions and shared the money with those in need. They worshipped together at the temple each day, met in homes for the Lord's Supper and shared their meals with great joy and generosity. **Acts 2:42, 47**

In a later passage it reads:
All the believers were united in heart and mind. And they felt that what they owned was not their own, so they shared everything they had. The apostles testified powerfully to the resurrection of the Lord Jesus and God's great blessing was upon them all. There were no needy people among them because those who owned land or houses would sell them and bring the money to the apostles to give to those in need. **Acts 4:32-35**

The social and economic organization of the early church is a clear indication of the common ownership preached in socialism, yet it was sustained by the ethical nature of the people, that is, the power of the Holy Spirit, who is the nature of God alive in man. Now most people argue that our society has become too complex for such a system and that practice was not meant to last for always. Firstly our society is not complex; only greed and the gigantic market economy it has created is. Capitalism depends only on the exploitation of the very poor for the benefit of the very rich. This system is directly denounced by Jesus and we see the fruits of the economy under the directive of God; one that is not directed by the excessive greed for private property. And if we say the church has evolved from this, we simply say it has moved away from God.

John Wesley

To say Christians did this only till the destruction of Jerusalem, is not true; for many did it long after. Not that there was any positive command for so doing: it needed not; for love constrained them. It was a natural fruit of that love wherewith each member of the community loved each other as his own soul. And if the whole Christian church had continued in this spirit, this usage must have continued through all ages. To affirm therefore that Christ did not design it should continue is neither more or less than to affirm that Christ did not design this measure of love should continue. I see no proof of this.

Since we profess that love is the only law in Christianity; it is this love and the generosity it yields as opposed to greed and selfishness that was the foundation of the early church's socialism. We have discussed how wealth is one of the key cornerstones of leaders; it is how they maintain their foothold, yet we have seen a different kind of leadership, the Servant-Leader, Pacifist and now Socialist. It is not the socialism that is brought about by the violent revolution of Marxism but one that comes about through the directive of the inner law of God that drives us to give to the needy and remember the forgotten. Private property is protected by law and even by the Jewish law, yet an egalitarian society was advocated in the early church. The Apostle Paul wrote, *'our desire is not that others might be relieved while you are hard pressed, but that there might be equality'*, (Corinthians 8:13). The early church provided a blueprint for that perfect equality sustained by the perfection of God, which is the answer to our ethical dilemma.

New Possibilities

Throughout time mankind has sought the walls of wisdom to find a perfect political theory. To Plato the philosopher kings were the only hope for a just society, the enlightenment thinkers rooted for a government by the people and for the people, some great monarchies were stripped of their powers and left almost as decorative, democracy has been hailed through all corners of the earth as the hope for a utopia and others even champion for anarchy-no authority, no hierarchy, no governments. For those who challenge existing powers they find revolution either through violence or activism is the answer to loosen the iron grip of despotic rulers, yet when we look at the issue of governance upon the earth it is important to state this law, *"power corrupts and absolute power corrupts absolutely"*. Our history has given us sufficient evidence of this; humans have failed in this business of ruling others because our nature corrupts us. History has shown us what is wrong with our governments; their reliance on force to keep order, their extravagance in the face of poverty and their self-exaltation. No new political theories will change these facts because none of them can change human nature; the success of governments relies on the ethical standing of those in power. Yet God offers hope in another kingdom under the directive of Him who is King of kings.

The Kingship of God and its Priesthood are inextricably linked. When Christ was nailed to the cross, He was as a King reclaiming His kingdom and a High Priest performing the cleansing ceremony for His people for all time, past, present and future. Righteousness and Justice are the foundations of God's Kingdom. Christ is Melchizedeck of whom it is written, *"And Melchizedeck king of Salem brought out bread and wine. (He was priest of God Most High)...and Abram gave him a tenth of everything"*, (Genesis 13:18-20). This King gave bread and wine, showing how salvation was tied to His government. Salem itself means Peace. It is a heavenly kingdom bought of God's blood and occupied by the ransomed.

Christian theology offers us a way to view the world in a possible perfect state, a state that may seem naive and out of touch with the complexity of society and diversity of culture. Yet as a religion based on faith, it is the belief in the seemingly impossible that is the foundation. The idea that we could stand by a utopia world of perfect leaders, no wars, just and equal societies seems like a romantic notion; but these beliefs have been the driving force of great movements for change throughout history. They have put an end to slavery and inspired racial equality and in our times of moral ambiguity, social and economic strain we must again look towards this perfect hope that in Christ we can have a world without oppression, war, poverty, suffering and it can be our new normal.

RIGHTS AND FREEDOM

H

uman rights have featured widely on the world stage in the past decades; there are outcries far and wide for the world to uphold and recognize the dignity and freedom of all people. Freedom stands at the centre of human rights reasoning; the ordinary person must be protected from the far reaching power of the state which seems always ready to crush them under its iron fist whether ideologically or physically. The individual must be freed from the chains that wish to tie the mind from liberty, tie the self from the freedom to be and so forth. The United Declaration of Human Rights was formed at the backdrop of a global society that had witnessed great evils under two very destructive world wars, had witnessed and was still continuing to witness the pernicious ways of overbearing governments and empires that daily denied the rights of the poor, the natives and the minorities. At the same time it was a society which was influenced by reason, it is reason that continues to be grounded as the basis of human rights thinking and reason still that is thought to safeguard and protect the innate dignity of the being. Humanists will ground human rights thinking in the material world, it is advancement in science and technology that will one day free the world from the disease of evil it is thought. Yet this diagnosis does not do justice to the dilemma that mankind is in. To understand what human rights and freedom are, we must look at mankind's history from the fall to the redemption because therein lies the diagnosis of society.

Human rights are assertions of human dignity; a dignity that is everywhere threatened by others. Often in the human rights discourse, there is a dichotomy between the victims and perpetrators .i.e. those who violate the rights of others and those whose rights are violated. It is imperative however to trace the disease of mankind at the fall. It is freedom therefore that stands at the heart of human rights thinking and it is always freedom that is at the core of Christian belief. God formed the Jewish nation from slaves that He saved from the oppressive Egyptians; Egypt itself was a symbol of sin, the original rights violator. At the same time Christ died in order to save all of God's people; from Adam to the last man; from the bondage of sin and its death. In essence to free us from the nature that made oppression of others possible and in other societies even honourable. The preceding sections have looked at the essence of man under sinful nature and the essence of man being built up by God, the man designed by God and according to God's will and nature. We have located this human free from the bondage of evil, this human transforming through the inner evolution, the moral revolution, we have spotted this being free from the oppression of political systems that rely on violence to assert peace and freedom; we have in essence located this human FREE. It has already been stated that we live in a binary world of two natures at war with each other and that the power of sin which we are born under was defeated by Christ at the cross granting us the *freedom* to act according to God's will which also means being able to uphold the rights of others.

It is important to go back to the history of humanity and to realize that the origin of the issue of human rights lies at the fall of man and at the nature that births chaos, the chaos we fight to correct. This is the diagnosis and the prognosis of what ails our world. It is in the context of our relationship with God and with each other that we find the antidote. Mankind finds dignity in the fact that it was created by God and in His image. It is within the Imago Dei that humans find their worth. The American Declaration of Independence states that it is *"equally and self-evidently all people are endowed by their Creator with certain unalienable Rights, that among these are Life, Liberty and the Pursuit of Happiness"*. Dr Charles Malik one of the key actors in drafting the UDHR stated, *"finally there is the question of their (human rights) origin. Where do they come from? Are they conferred upon me by some external visible power such as the state or the United Nations, so that what is now granted me may someday be conceivably withdrawn from me? Or do they belong to my essence so that if they are violated in any way I cease to be a human being at all? If they did belong to my essence, should they not also be grounded in a Supreme Being who, by being the Lord of history, could guarantee their meaning and stability?"* The Imago Dei underlines our claim over justice. It is within our origin that we find the answer to our being, *"without God, it is impossible to uphold human value and worth objectively",*(Wilson). It is within the logos that the worth of mankind is again ascertained, because it is the Word of God that died for mankind, granting that the life of mankind was worth the sacrifice. It is not the evolutionary process that grants humans worth, for the grounds of man's worth under that argument are iffy and history has shown how science has been used to explain away the dignity and worth of humans. The origin of mankind allows us to locate all humans as brothers and sisters made by God, coming from one womb of Eve at the same time all creation is made one and equal by Christ at the cross.

When asked what the most important law was Jesus answered, *"the most important commandment is this: 'Listen O Israel! The Lord our God is the one and only Lord. And you must love the Lord your God with all your heart, all your soul, all your mind, and all your strength.' The second is equally important: 'Love your neighbour as yourself.' No other commandments are greater than these,"* (Mark 12:29-31). The fall of man cut humanity off from God and tainted relations with others, yet Jesus states that humanity must go back to God and must reconcile with each other, this is the only way to achieve universal peace and harmony. This also is the basis of human rights thinking. If all people loved others as they loved themselves, then it would be easy to follow the Golden Rule: do unto others as you would have them do to you. If this was followed then we would all uphold the worth of others and therefore their rights. The Jewish law was founded upon these two commandments stated above. If mankind loved God and followed Him, that love would be demonstrated by their love for other people as well, where that prevails, there would be no demeaning of others. The drafter of the 1948 Universal Declaration of Human Rights (UDHR), Rene Samuel Cassin, Nobel Peace Prize Laureate, embedded these values in the first Article of the UDHR which begins with the statement, *"we should act towards one another in a spirit of brotherhood."* He explained this corresponds with two biblical injunctions which state that, *'love thy neighbour as thyself'* and *'you shall not oppress a stranger, for you once were strangers.'* Carl Henry argues that, *"the theological basis for evangelical involvement in public justice is located in God's creation ethic and His universal revelation including the imago Dei that, however sullied, nonetheless survives the Fall...Social responsibility is not a responsibility that derives one-sidedly on Christians...Responsibility for justice in the social order is as universal as the human race. Social justice is due from all persons to all persons."*

The commandment to love the Lord your God is closely tied to truth and morality which are also tied to freedom and justice. *"Without God, man loses his bearing in this world and he cannot find them again till he has found the One whose world it is. God made our life and God alone can tell us its meaning,"* (J.I Packer). And what does this mean? It is to live in love and communion with all others and how is this made possible? Through living in communion with God first, who first authored our worth when He made us in His image and then again when He remade us at the cross into His perfection; His perfect Image. Freedom lies at the centre of the Christian doctrine and it is first of all freedom to know God and freedom to be like God that brings about all other freedoms. The cross is a symbol of one Man's suffering meant to end all suffering; one Man's humiliation meant to exalt all mankind. And this exaltation is the ability to live and act according to God's will, set free from the bondage of the ignorance that once made us blind to the inherent dignity of all people and made visible distinctions not really existent. *"There is no longer Jew or Gentile, slave or free, male and female. For you are all one in Christ,'*-(Galatians 3:28). Luther wrote, *"as our heavenly father has in Christ freely come to our aid, we also ought freely to help our neighbour through our body and works, and each should become as it were a Christ to the Other that we may be Christs to one another and Christ may be the same in all."*

There is an inextricable link between rights and morality. Human rights make a claim to truths that are universal .i.e. moral standards that are true in all societies at all times. In a culturally diverse world, it is difficult to assert universal standards unless we are also asserting moral absolutes. Therefore the idea of human rights is grounded in universalism, morals and truths which are independent of context dependent interpretation and are inviolate. It is impossible to make such claims independent of an All Knowing Deity, who too is the author of the absolute truth; the logos. Therefore human rights assertions can only be true if it is also true that there is a Universal God governing the Universal Natural Law, who Himself is that Law which we aim to apply within the contexts of our world, independent of our interpretations and incorruptible. If we cannot assert this then we cannot uphold the law. Our duties towards God are aligned to our understanding of the Universal Truth, it is from these truths that we learn what we owe to each other .i.e. to love our neighbour as self, to do to others as we want to be done to us. The whole Jewish law was based upon the fact that God is truth and that truth was to guide humanity in their relations with each other; these are the same assertions the drafters of the UDHR drew from, that the truth of universal brotherhood as evident in the bible is a moral absolute that is and must be true in all societies, to all people indiscriminately.

When the Jewish law was established it was understood as a universal law applying to all people, of all nations even though it was not so at the time. The law begins by asserting that the God that rescued the Israelites from Egypt was the only true God; it also followed that the moral standards He was giving to His people were Universal codes of conduct. Jesus states that *"do unto others as you want them to do to you, for this is the law and the prophets."* It is the law itself that Christ came to fulfil .i.e. to give all people the ability to love their neighbour as they love themselves. From the beginning of Christianity, universalism was at its heart. The early church tore down the barriers once dividing people, *'there is no Jew or Gentile, no slave or free, no male or female'* in Christ all are equal and all are one. We find here the assertions made in the UDHR, freedom and equality for all. We find that this is the purpose of the law. The ecumenical nature of the church shows the lack of nationalism in the Christian doctrine. On the day of Pentecost the disciples received the gift of tongues and they prayed in foreign languages, this drew the attention of foreigners who heard their own various languages spoken thus establishing a unity in Christ that transcended national and cultural borders. Today the world is plagued by issues such as xenophobia, racism, the neglect and oppression of migrants and refugees and the displacement of marginalized groups. At the heart of these issues is the separation we have made on the basis of nationality and race. At the onset of the creation of the Jewish nation, God made it clear that there was to be no distinction between the native and the traveller.

You shall not oppress the sojourner. You know the heart of a sojourner, for you were sojourners in the land of Egypt. **Exodus 23:9**

You shall have the same rule for the sojourner and for the native for I am the Lord your God. **Leviticus 24:22**

He executes justice for the fatherless and the widow, and loves the sojourner, giving him food and clothing. **Deuteronomy 10:18**

And when you reap the harvest of your land, you shall not reap your field right up to its edge, nor shall you gather the gleanings after your harvest. You shall leave them for the poor and for the sojourner. **Leviticus 23:22**

The ecumenical nature of the church is also tied to the freedom of thought that was at the centre of evangelism in the early church. In the face of extreme persecution, the early church clung to their freedom of conscience; which was their right to believe in the new doctrine of Christ so opposed to the dictates of the societies around them. This liberty is greatly tied to both truth and morality. It is the freedom to think, to question and even to have faith that leads to the freedom to know God and to act according to His will. We have already established that humans are not self-generative beings; they can neither generate good nor evil on their own but even if they do not have the free will to generate a nature, they are given a choice at least to choose which nature they are to be subject to; God's or not. It is this freedom of conscience that was at the centre of the growth and development of the early church as the church fought against opposing forces for the right to believe and the right to worship and it too asserted the world's right to this by abiding to its command not to judge the world but to love.

Rights of others are connected to the responsibilities and duties of others towards God. *"One person's religious duty not to kill, steal or bear false witness is another person's right to life, property and reputation as they are now protected by human rights law,"* (John Witte Jr). Religious instructions under the Jewish law and by the apostles were given as social responsibilities that all members of the community had towards each other. *"Be judges for the lowly one and the fatherless boy. To the afflicted one and the one of little means, do justice. Provide escape for the lowly one and the poor one. Out of the hand of the wicked ones, deliver them,"* (Psalms 82:3-4). In Proverbs 31:8-9 it reads, *"Open your mouth for the speechless one, in the cause of all those passing away. Open your mouth, judge righteously and plead the cause of the afflicted one and the poor one."* Thus God safeguards the rights of the lowly by commanding society to champion their rights. It is the moral obligation of all those who call themselves God's people to advocate for those who cannot do so for themselves, to stand up against evil and to stand for justice, to champion the cause of those with little rights and to help the orphans and widows. These responsibilities are at the centre of Jewish law and it is for the cause of the afflicted that Jesus died.

"The Spirit of the Sovereign Lord Jehovah is upon me for the reason that Jehovah has anointed me to tell good news to the meek ones. He has sent me to bind up the broken-hearted, to proclaim liberty to those taken captive and the wide opening (of the eyes) even to the prisoners, to proclaim the year of goodwill on the part of Jehovah," (Isaiah 61:1-2). This liberty also lies at the heart of human rights law. It is freedom from the excesses of the state that is the basis of human rights law, to ensure that the individual is safeguarded from the encroachment of the state in their lives. In a preceding section we have discussed how leadership under the Christian doctrine does away with all the oppression that has served to debase the individual and the systems therein that unjustly condemn, imprison and impoverish the ordinary people. However under the order of Christ it is freedom of liberty that characterizes the government and justice by which all people are governed. It is freedom first from the self and freedom from the excesses of world systems. *"Is not this the fast that I choose; to lose the bonds of wickedness, to undo the straps of the yoke, to let the oppressed go free and to break every yoke? Is it not to share your bread with the hungry and bring the homeless poor into your house; when you see the naked, to cover him, and not to hide yourself from your own flesh? ...if you pour yourself out for the hungry and satisfy the desire of the afflicted, then shall your light rise in the darkness and your gloom be as the noonday..."* (Isaiah 58:6-12). These verses recapitulate the religious requirements of God to His people, which are essentially to safeguard the rights, needs, freedoms and liberties of others. God states that this is the true fast. The religious anti-slavery protests of the 19th century, the recovery from the Holocaust and the civil rights activism of Rev Dr Martin Lurther King are some of the historical examples of how these religious ideals have been used to champion for the rights of the oppressed and afflicted.

Social justice was the cornerstone of Jewish religious law, such that in Matthew 25:35 Jesus states that he who helps the least has helped

God also. The law protected the rights of workers, widows and orphans and God equated religious purity to the fulfilment of these commands. In Jeremiah 22:13 God states, *"woe to him who builds his house by unrighteousness, and his upper rooms by injustice, who makes his neighbour serve him for nothing and does not give him his wages."* The same rights of workers are safeguarded by the International Labour Organization and the UDHR. To his people God commands, *"learn to do good, seek justice, correct oppression, bring justice to the fatherless, plead the widow's cause,"* (Isaiah 1:17). In another passage it reads, *"Religion that is pure and undefiled before God the father is this; to visit the orphans and widows in their affliction..."* (James 1:27). The rights of children are safeguarded in the United Nations Convention on the Rights of Children.

As above mentioned the rights of others to life are safeguarded by others' religious duty not to kill. Furthermore the non-violent nature of the Christian doctrine cements the rights to life as well as freedom from violence. The Christian commands to not return evil with evil and to turn the other cheek ensure that the world becomes more harmonious, peaceful and free from all forms of violence including war, thereby safeguarding the right to life. Proverbs 24:11 commands us to, *"deliver those who are being taken away to death and those staggering to the slaughter."*

The human rights heritage has become so engrained within our culture, yet it has its origins within the Judeo-Christian ethics. The moral foundations laid out by God for His people have been a light house in the dark path of human history. The rich ethics of Christianity have become the spring and fountainhead of today's moral foundations. There is not only a correlation between religion and human rights, but human rights are derived directly from religious ethics. It is from their religious roots also that they derive their meaning and strength, torn away from that original cloth, there is a danger of plunging into nihilism. The freedom offered by Judeo-Christian ethics with regards to the individual and how he or she ought to be treated by the collective and ought to act as a member of the collective is closely tied to truth as well as responsibility. It is in knowing God, our duty towards Him and His children that human rights law was founded and strengthened. Thus it is in the best of humanity that we find the handiwork of God in His plan to create a perfect world of His design and essence.

CONCLUSION

The Kingdom of God in Us

I will liken the journey of mankind on earth to an endless search for the answers to an equation. We are in a process of solving a mathematical problem, like with math, we are looking for the laws of nature. Some of us reach answers that make sense to us and we believe those to be the laws but the answers are not human inventions; they do not come about through our reasoning, they are not our handiwork but they are discoveries of things that already exist. The answer is God. Mathematics shows the path we must take in searching for the answer; we must relentlessly pursue the truth; the one and only answer and not settle for the imperfect just because it quenches our ego; but the beauty of mathematics is that it aims to perfection. 1 plus 1 equals 2 is beautiful because it is true and because of that, it is perfect. This is the same as our search for the answers to the issues of what plague our world; we are in search for the perfect truth; for that **one** correct answer. We are on a journey of discovery; what we look for is written in natural laws; it is already there and we must just reach out to it and embrace it. And if our minds are used to excess; toil and labour find it hard to believe that the answer could be so simple and the labour for it so little yet the prize itself so priceless; then in that moment our minds must also embrace the amazing fact that it is not by anything we have done that the world is made whole but it is by the Grace of God. This same God lives in us and has made His home in us and in our hearts; there His Kingdom reigns and we are called to exhibit His glory in the world He calls to Him.

Jesus Christ is placed like a fulcrum in history, holding all things in place. He is the cornerstone, without which nothing makes sense and through which all things are created. He existed in the beginning as the Word of God by which all things were created and at the cross He became the Living bread of God, the Word by which the fallen inner world of man was remade, exalted and made perfect; into the perfect image of God. All history stands at attention before the cross as it is there that all events throughout time come together and are given meaning. The cross is the washbasin of God; it is His paintbrush, His breath given once more to mankind. It is at the cross that God stands as the Great Law maker rewriting the Laws of the Universe that had been corrupted in Eden, yet it is not to Eden that God recalls mankind; it is to the grave of Jesus that all man are called to lay down and die and it is from the waters that Christ rose from that all creation is called to rise again. At the cross we witness the Great remaking of all creation; the cross stands as the end of time and the beginning. By the cross, God judged the end of the reign of darkness and the genesis of the kingdom of Light. The kingdom that was birthed by the disobedience of Adam and Eve was defeated, the cross there stands through all time, past, present and future and by the blood of Jesus the Kingdom of darkness with its Laws that darkened history and separated man from God and each other was erased and its power which allowed it to make slaves of God's children was made obsolete. It is at the cross that God's Law became alive in the kingdom of man and there we see His Word spoken once and echoing throughout all time and that echo dressing the dry bones of His creation with flesh; holy flesh that is seen fit to endure eternity with God. It is the Kingdom of God that was placed in all those who confess Jesus as their Saviour; the Kingdom alive in us as the promise of things to come.

This essay has been written to try to capture what the Kingdom of God as given to us in the history of God's walk with humanity is. We have seen that the spiritual force existing within humans lies at the centre of what our history has been like. It is our nature; our natural inclinations that colour the face of our world. Yet this nature is also a Law existing in a universe outside the human universe yet controlling it. We have discovered that mankind cannot exist in a spiritual vacuum because mankind cannot generate nature i.e. we cannot produce good or evil on our own thus Adam and Eve's disobedience towards God made alive in us the nature of sin and our sinful nature tainted history. The nature alive in us is the very opposite of God's nature and we have witnessed this nature in the unjust ways we treat each other, in the oppressive and tyrannical acts of our governments and although we have attempted to thwart this nature through laws and mass movements, it acts as a power alive in us and this power can only be overcome if its hold over us is made obsolete and we allow another Law, another Nature to make its home in us. We have witnessed the Law, the Word of God by which we are made alive and that word is Christ who at the cross laid all history at His feet and made obsolete the power of the nature of Satan at work in the world. It is the inner remaking of mankind through redemption that is the hope for our world, that recreation is the transformation of the inner man into the image of God; it is God who takes residence in the vessel that was once occupied by sinful nature. We are called to be God's vessels and to exercise His Law within our hearts. This cessation of the power of darkness is the hope for justice and peace in the world. God walked with the Israelites in order to herald His kingdom through them; to reveal to them the nature they had lost and it is through that journey from Eden to Calvary that we learn of God's nature; His Law. Whilst we have systematically confined God to religion, the reality of His walk with Israel defies this confinement. He showed Himself as the Holiness which all mankind is to emulate, the same holiness that is the guide to our moral standards, by which we understand the laws we make for ourselves and the ends to which they are made. At the same time He showed Himself as the One true King of all the earth, whose Kingdom would overturn empires off their hinges and govern the ages. Yet His kingdom is not of this world He confesses because it is a kingdom functioning under a law opposite to the ones that govern our own. He is the King who is Lord over all the Universe and Creator of all things, yet He is a humble servant to the people He leads, to Him leadership and service are the same thing. He too is the defender of His people and the Highest Law of His Kingdom is love; He is the Protector of the rights of His people, the very people He has made His treasure boxes, tasked to preserve the honour and dignity of others as though they were defending their own and God's.

God through His Word presents to us a picture of a perfect world, it is the world He has been weaving throughout time, a world of peace, harmony and love yet that Kingdom in all its perfection remains like threads hanging upon a loom, these seemingly disorderly threads can only make sense if woven together with the scarlet thread that is Christ Himself, He is the centrepiece in all; without which life is meaningless and hope is vacant. The kingdom of God with all its vast promises of a new Golden Age is not possible without salvation, without the recreation of mankind into the image of God. He is the God who declares that human laws can never bring about complete change because they wrestle with a nature alive in man, yet He promises a Law that will live in the Hearts of His people; this Law is God Himself. Yet how can we achieve this perfection without salvation? We can only continue in our own institutions and search in vain for justice. God promises an end to war and violence yet how can this power die inside us without the power that can save? We continue to look to violence to bring peace. God promises equality for all people, yet our nature is corrupt and greedy, how can we sacrifice ourselves to help others if not for the active power of Christ in us? God promises a Kingdom in which He rules as the King of Justice and Peace-the Servant King, yet how can we sustain this if our nature is corrupted? The kingdom of God rests upon righteousness without which even the most perfect ideals are corrupted and this righteousness we speak of is the righteousness of God Himself which we have been granted by Christ at the cross. Humanists will hinge the hope of the world on our own abilities, the strength of our will, our intelligence and our supposed goodness but the problem of evil in the world is everyone's problem because the power alive in the institutions we label as our oppressors is alive in us as well. Humans have no goodness to speak of because no amount of human goodness can break the power of the nature alive in us. The problem of the world is a problem of nature and only the wisdom of God has paved a way to make that nature obsolete no amount of human intelligence can break the curse of sin. It is only the active Law of God that can banish the law active in the world today and that Law has been at the cross suspended throughout all time and recreating all who will respond to its call and enter even here on earth the Kingdom of God.

The Holy Kingdom of God is alive and active in us; the fullness of God and His Christ is made active in those who confess Jesus as their Messiah. The active power of the Holy Spirit has made it possible for the righteousness of God to live in us; for the active power of God's Law to work in us; to change our nature. And if our nature changes it means there is hope for the world; a world governed by peace, justice and love. God alone is the Hope for the troubled and crippled world we live because by His Word He spoke the vast Universe into being and by that same Word He made a way for the Light to overcome darkness (tyranny, war, hunger, destitution, inequality, discrimination, injustice). Therefore there is no logical justification for our assertion that the doctrine of Christ has no place in the social, political and economic makeup of the world because it is the **answer**, the **one** and **only truth** revealed to us yet still waiting to be discovered. Men and women of prudence and wisdom will recognize it for what it is; it is the essence of our **being** and **Being** itself.

PART THREE

THE BUILDERS OF THE HOUSE

A Defence of Christian involvement in public policy

"Universalistic egalitarianism, from which sprang the ideals of freedom and a collective life in solidarity, the autonomous conduct of life and emancipation, the individual morality of conscience, human rights and democracy, is the direct legacy of the Judaic ethic of justice and the Christian ethic of love. This legacy, substantially unchanged, has been the object of continual critical appropriation and reinterpretation. To this day, there is no alternative to it. And in light of the current challenges of a post-national constellation, we continue to draw on the substance of this heritage. Everything else is just idle postmodern talk,"

Jurgen Habermas- Time of Transitions

CHRISTIAN MANDATE FOR SOCIAL INVOLVEMENT

T

he separation of the church and the state', that is the phrase most penned for the justification of the confinement of religion in the private sphere. Enlightenment thinkers and philosophers have argued for the removal of church principles in the governing of the public sphere. The belief is that religious epistemology is not relevant to explain the real world and at best these principles since they are not held by all people and secondly not open to those who do not adhere to them are not healthy and are counterproductive if not damaging to public policy conversation. It is reason 'superior' to religion that must be the driver of public policy conversations and actions, is the argument. This section will examine the history of Christianity from the ancient Jewish law and religion arguing that in Jewish society there was no separation between religion and public policy and that far from being irrational, religious precepts were put in place to respond to actual moral and social problems for which public policy is put in place. Secondly, it will argue that religion offers values and principles that inform not only our relations with God but also our relations with each other. A close examination of the evolution of Christianity from its Hebrew heritage shows the close link between faith, reason and action.

The widespread view that religion should have no place in public policy has its roots in the Enlightenment era and has been cemented by various arguments over the years. The Enlightenment thought that religion should not go beyond the private sphere has been heavily supported today in everyday discourse and by thinkers such as John Rawls and Richard Rorty. In his 1994 paper *Religion as Conversation stopper,* Rorty argues that we cannot '*keep a democratic political community going unless religious believers remain willing to trade privatization for a guarantee of religious liberty.*' He seems to believe that the pluralistic world we live in requires the separation of the public and private spheres in matters of faith. Locke on his part believed that religious organizations are primarily involved in issues of worship and the salvation of the souls. It is the otherworldly matters that religion focuses on and other matters to do with the material world are the domain of the state, so the argument goes. There seems to be an assumption that religion and the issues it addresses are completely withdrawn from the physical world of men; as if religion is only for the inner man and has nothing to say about and to the outer being within a community. This however could not be further from the truth. As William Sweet puts it, *'although faith or religious belief involves assent to a series of beliefs, those beliefs are both descriptive (.i.e. have a relation to this world and not just to a reality which is beyond the empirical, observable and material) and have an expressive role or function in a person's life.'* In essence; religious faith involves a call to social action.

The argument for the confinement of religion to the private sphere assumes that *that* is its natural domain, that a step away from the private world is not only a violation of the *social and political rules* but also a violation of religious rules. A minute examination of religious history provides sufficient evidence to lay this argument to rest however. From the onset of God's walk with people the spiritual was always tied to the political, social, economic, Judicial and personal life. Belief in God for the Hebrews was not compartmentalized in a different department from the material and empirical world as others would have us believe. The issues that religion dealt with permeated from the way neighbour treated neighbour, all the way to the political affairs of the king and his officials. In fact the infant Jewish nation was ruled by God as king for centuries before the first Hebrew king Saul was put in place. The judges ruled the people under the direct instruction of God; the spiritual had everything to do with the everyday affairs regarding civil wellbeing. The divine principles of God were not merely for the 'salvation of the soul' as Locke thought; they dealt with human affairs and how people lived together and treated each other. In fact it was only when one lived rightly with their neighbours and sought for social justice that the religious task was said to have been rightly accomplished.

The idea that religious organizations have no place in public life because they deal with otherworldly affairs is reductionist. Religions must be allowed to explain themselves to the world and not for the world to define and confine them in boxes they do not fit. God did not deal with men only for their private gain but also for the collective, national and international gain. The mouthpiece of God was the law, the law that advocated for a better and more just world. God sought to purify His people so that when they attained the holiness of God, they would not only receive salvation but also learn the secret to living together in harmony. The Sermon on the Mount is one such example of God's plight. Jesus teaches generosity, pacifism, sacrifice and love; principles that when followed changed the world touched by the early church greatly. The prophets of the Old Testament acted as beacons of God's justice, the advocates for a better world advocated by the law; a just and egalitarian world without oppression or strife. *'Is this not the fast I want, that you take care of the widows and orphans?'* This is God's plight to His people. Thus the assumption that religion does not act to protect civil interests reflects little understanding of what true religion is. The empirical and material world is the concern of God and His followers. God is both priest and king, and it is through His righteousness that He builds a better and perfect world as king of justice and peace. Justice and peace are of concern to a world coloured by injustice and chaos and therefore do not apply to a heavenly kingdom (assumed to be the only concern of religion) which is perfect but in fact applies to our imperfect and chaotic world. Believers are therefore called to build up this kingdom of justice and peace.

Those who argue for the removal of the religious discourse from the public sphere state that religious principles are based on assumptions not shared by others. They seem to assume that all non-religious principles are in agreement with each other; which is really not the case. The argument that in a pluralistic world the religious discourse has no place is self-defeating because in a truly pluralistic world all voices deserve an audience. Why then should the religious voice be an exception? The assumption is also that religious discourse is opposite all other discourses and causes discord and should be banished; ignoring the contribution of Christianity to the development of Western culture and the modern world as we know it. In a multi-vocal world, the voice of religion should be permitted to be what it is and not what others would have it be. Having said so, the separation of the public and the private sphere is alien to Christian beliefs as is demonstrated not only by its rich and vibrant history of social involvement but also by its very principles.

The Christ who lives in us is High Priest, King, Judge, Defender, Peacemaker and He commands us to be His hands and feet; to build His kingdom according to His design. The Christian doctrine negates confinement to the private sphere. *'You are the light of the world and the light should not be put under a basket'*, Jesus states. Christ arranges our inner selves so that we may in turn direct the outer world. God speaks of politics when Jesus tells His followers to be servants of the world if they wanted to be just leaders. Jesus speaks of economic justice when He tells the rich to give to the poor and this was demonstrated by the communal living of the early church. God speaks of social justice when He calls us to champion the cause of the needy, the marginalized, the oppressed, the orphans, the widows and the imprisoned. Jesus championed justice and peace when He denounced violence and when He sacrificed His life for sinners He acted as Judge and Lawmaker, writing His laws into the heart of those who believe.

The church is not only concerned with otherworldly issues as Locke will have it, it is also involved in the public life that aims at the wellbeing of all people and justice in the world. Having thus said, for the individual Christian there is a call to acting according to what they believe in. It is a call to not only act according to private convictions but also the convictions of a community; a community that if and when it acts as one can impact the world around it in a positive way and essentially build up the kingdom of God and His house.

THE EARLY CHURCH: FORESHADOW OF A WORLD TO COME

Throughout the history of mankind** no movement has been more influential and beneficial to humanity than Christianity and within the crucible of its own peculiar history no era stands out more than the early church. It stands out like a mountain reaching up to touch heaven itself amidst the hilly cluster of the later church's many compromises. The testimony it has left us of the power of Christ and His Holy Spirit and the vision of God's will for the world that it exhibits allows us to look upon it as upon an everlasting hope. From it reverberates the empowering and enduring words and works of the apostles and the early fathers; Words that echo and shake the world with their truth even if the world and the modern church may attempt to drown them within the tempest of their doctrines. Its works too will always shine a light upon us to follow in this indifferent world and they still condemn the modern church of sleeping on the job entrusted to us by God; to reflect His love to the world; to build His house. This section will look at the early church and its unwavering commitment to social justice and charity, evidence that it is not only the duty of the church but it is also the will of God that His church becomes the salt and light of the world.

Undoubtedly the church had humble beginnings, started by Jesus, a humble carpenter from Galilee. The uninspired eye would see nothing hopeful in His prospects from an earthly point of view; however the Jewish history had much to say of Him, for it is Him who held the promise of a better world, the Messiah. Though His ministry lasted for only 3 years the influence He made during His life; His words, His works will always be the foundation and example of the church. The Sermon on the Mount still remains the moral code of the church and the foundation upon which even the Human Rights laws were established. Crucified on a lowly cross Jesus would rise as the first born of God's new creation, the fulfilment and the evidence of the promise, the hope in the flesh and then ascending as the Supreme

Deity to the heavens. Those who were left would look to Him, to His salvation power as the example of what God wills us to do and also as the power and confidence that it can be done. It is upon Jesus, healer of the sick, comforter of the hurting, friend of sinners, lover of the marginalized and infringed, friend of women and children, peacemaker, humble Master and God, justice and Saviour that the early church looked to for moral guidance. And when they looked upon Him diligently and truly, they suffered greatly but they transformed the world they touched tremendously.

The early church broke down the divide between the rich and poor, slaves and free, men and women, Jews and Gentiles. We find in the scriptures reference of the early church's new social organization. The apostles' teachings manifested themselves in action, the faith of the early church was not merely a private faith but it also came naturally with outward fruits of that faith as the apostle James said, faith without works is dead.

All the believers devoted themselves to the apostles' teachings and to fellowship, and to sharing in meals (including the Lord's Supper) and to prayer. A deep sense of awe came over them all, and the apostles performed many miraculous signs and wonders. And all the believers met together in one place and shared everything they had. They sold their property and possessions and shared the money with those in need. They worshipped together at the temple each day, met in homes for the Lord's Supper and shared their meals with great joy and generosity. **Acts 2:42, 47**

A description of Christians for heathens written around AD 125 in Athens states it was the Christian custom to take strangers into one's home and rejoice over them as if they were brothers and sisters. A book by a Christian martyr in Italy AD 165 records, *'we who hated and destroyed one another and on account of their different manners would not live with men of a different tribe, now since the coming of Christ, live familiarly with them.'* Clement wrote that the Christian morality obliges us to '*love strangers not only as friends and relatives but as ourselves, both in body and soul... Accordingly, it is expressly said, 'thou shalt not abhor an Egyptian, for thou wast a sojourner in Egypt.'* Compare the early church's response to strangers to our response to the growing refugee crisis in the world. God's message to Peter regarding Cornelius and subsequently all Gentiles as well as Paul's work among the Gentiles was key to bridging the gap between people of different races, proclaiming and cementing the universal brotherhood of the church regardless of race or creed.

The early church is credited for giving children visibility in the world and also for ending infanticide. Jesus' treatment of and teachings regarding children led to the forbidding of ancient practices that permitted parents to leave their unwanted or undesired children in dumps, on hillsides to die of exposure; be torn by wild animals or selling them into slavery. Members of the early church took these abandoned children as their own until infanticide was no more. Norwegian scholar Bakke wrote a study of Jesus' impact on this issue titled simply: When Children Became People: the Birth of Childhood in Early Christianity.

The Early Christians: In their own words- Eberhard Arnold

The believers put their hearts and soul into acts of love. The freedom of self-determination in their work gave an entirely voluntary character to all social work done by the early Christians. Hermas described the spirit ruling in the church. He said the wealthy could be fitted in the building of the church only after they had stripped themselves of their wealth for the sake of their poorer brothers and sisters...In general material goods were seen as common property just like light, air, water, soil and other natural necessities. The practice of surrendering everything in love was the hallmark of the Christians. When this declined it was seen as the loss of the Spirit of Christ.

Urged by this love many sold themselves into slavery or went to debtor's prison for the sake of others...In fact everything that the church owned at that time belonged to the poor. The affairs of the poor were the affairs of the church; it supported bereft women and children, the sick and the destitute...To help others the Christians took the hardest privations upon themselves and never limited their works of love. Even Emperor Julian had to admit that, 'the godless Galileans feed our poor in addition to their own.'...Everyone was equally respected, equally judged and equally called. The result was equality and fellowship in everything; the same rights, the same obligation to work, the same opportunities...The mutual respect among those early Christians bore fruit in a socialistic solidarity rooted in a love that sprang from the belief in the equality of all people...The rank afforded by property and profession was recognized to be incompatible with such fellowship and simplicity and repugnant to it. For that reason alone the early Christian had an aversion to any high judicial positions and commission in the army. They found it impossible to take responsibility for any penalty or imprisonment, any disenfranchisement, any judgement over life or death or the execution of any death sentence pronounced by martial or criminal courts.

Saint Augustine of Hippo (354-430)

The superfluities of the rich are the necessities of the poor. When you possess superfluity, you possess what belongs to others. God gives the world to the poor as well as to the rich. Redouble your charity. For, on account of the things which each one of us possesses singly, wars exist, hatreds, discords, strives among human beings, tumults, dissensions, scandals, sins, injustices and murders. Why? Do we fight over the things we possess in common? We inhale this air in common with others; we all see the sun in common.

A new kind of humanity was in the making and with it a new radical world; a world drawing its design from the teachings and example of Jesus, the work of the apostles and the power of the Holy Spirit under the directive of God. The faith of the early church as can be seen was not merely for private affirmation and although they considered themselves as citizens of the heavenly kingdom first, their duty was also as ambassadors of that kingdom on earth. They did not seek to conquer the worldly kingdom with armies or might, but through their love they were able to turn around centuries old customs and practices, they were able to bring together different races and creeds under the single title of children of God. In the house of God there seized to be rich or poor, powerful or weak, men or women, slave or free. The early church had arrived where all the world strives to be; its society was beyond egalitarian, it was pacifist, humanitarian and just. The church reveals to us the answer. Every year nations and international bodies spend billions of dollars trying to build a world such as that which the church had built yet still the world aims to banish the light from the public sphere and the church seems to not comprehend the immense and world altering power it possesses.

If anything the early church is proof of the great error made when people assert that the church has no place in the public sphere for with it is the privatization of the hope of the world. The early church even under extreme persecution exhibited the tremendous glory of God. Drawing its roots from the ancient Jewish tradition derived from God's law to treat all people equally, to stand up for the least in society, we see under the banner of the church everyone exalted, everyone granted worth, everyone remembered, we see everyone raised to the same level such that there existed no caste or class system. We can confidently look at the early church as the hope that the Kingdom of God is here and not merely coming. The Kingdom of God lives in every believer of the gospel, within us lives the full power of God, the transformative power that exalts the poor and humbles the great, the power that ends poverty and wars.

Given the message of the church and the work it has done for the good of humanity it is a wonder why there is insistence that it be confined to the margins of the world and more still why the church remains reluctant to follow the teachings of Christ to the fullest. From the onset the church was understood as the possession of God, its literal meaning is *that which belongs to God*. The early church thrived not because it was popular with the world, but because it was not. It was different in every aspect, its members held on to ideals that were regarded by the world as reflections of weakness, ideals such as humility, charity, pacifism, yet though the church was exclusive in its beliefs, its love and charity were not. Whilst the unbelievers abandoned their sick in times of plagues the church nurtured those sick regardless of the fact that they did not share their faith, they suffered with them and died with them. Within its love and its works we see God exhibited to us, His handiwork displayed for all the world, past, present and future-so that within it we can see God's magnificent plan for the world-a world without war, hunger, disease, class or discrimination. And as the church looks upon it and diligently sees the plan that God has for His world through us; we can take a stand and begin to build the kingdom of God realizing that the power of God exhibited by the early church is not a thing of history but the same power to love and change the world lives in us too. It is not for the world to tell the church where it should begin and end, nor is it for the world to confine the church in the private world. This is ahistorical, the Christian faith has always come with the mandate for social transformation- this is the kingdom of God presaged by the early church.

CHRISTIANITY
The foundation of western culture

T

he **Western society has a culture of humanitarianism,** holds ideals of freedom of the individual, of equality and justice, ideals that make up the core of their being, that define their very essence, and ideals that they have held as banners to the world and willed it to follow their moral compass. Yet whilst the world highly praises these ideals and wills itself to honour them, they little or at all acknowledge the fact that these ideals not only originate from the Judeo-Christian ethics, they were derived from them. The history of Christianity is so interwoven within the history of Western development such that it is impossible to remove Christian influence from it without in turn obliterating the western world culturally, morally, legally, scientifically and socially. As we turn the pages of history we see written upon the founding pages of the Western world Christian men and women building its first schools, charting their moral path, writing their laws, starting their hospitals; creating literally, artistic, musical masterpieces that would define them for always; in essence building up their souls in ways that though they may deny their influence they cannot erase their mark upon them without in turn erasing all they are and all their history. It is not only fair but most true to state that not only did Christianity make the greatest impact upon the development of the Western world; it is essentially its very foundation.

'Contrary to the history texts' treatment of the subject, Christian influence on values, beliefs and practices in Western culture are abundant and well ingrained into the flourishing society of today' (Schmidt 2004). In the preceding sections we have explored the values of the Jews and Christians and God's will and directive for His people to champion for the lowly and poor; we have also seen how this mandate was carried out so perfectly by the early church. We may see the same ideals today in the societies we live and within International declarations such as the Human Rights Declarations, Convention of children's rights, women's

rights and so on and give little thought as to the religious origins of these rights. In fact it is astounding how popular discourse has come to regard religion as opposed to these rights when their origin lies within Judeo-Christian ethics; that too not indirectly but deriving directly from the words and actions of Jesus Christ. Western values and morals ride upon the tidal wave of Christian ethics. Human rights and the value of human life are derived directly from the teachings of Jesus as ethicist David P Gushee states, *'the justice teachings of Jesus are closely related to a commitment to life's sanctity.'* Thus at the dawn of the West's awakening into a civilized culture we find the deep belief in a transcendent value system as the cornerstone and foundation of their moral and cultural evolution. It is Christianity that turned them from the barbarism of human sacrifices, slavery, infanticide and it is Christianity that shaped their ideas of marriage and the family. The Western world did not become what it is today because of the ingenious of great men and women, no, when it was sculptured into a world, it was upon the design that Christianity laid before them that they attempted to mold themselves.

'The liberty and justice that are enjoyed by humans in Western societies and in some non-Western countries are increasingly seen as the products of a benevolent, secular government that is the provider of all things. There seems to be no awareness that the liberties and rights that are currently operative in free societies of the West are to a great degree the result of Christianity's influence' (Schmidt 2004). Jesus' treatment of women led directly to the elevation of the position of women in society including the Western society where Christianity spread. Jesus had women in His inner circle, His meeting with the Samaritan woman at the well, His anointing by Mary of Bethany, His friendship with Mary and Martha, His helping of Mary Magdalene, His public admiration of the poor widow who gave two copper coins, His healing of the woman with the issue of blood, the presence of His mother, Mary Magdalene and the other women at the crucifixion and His appearance

to Mary Magdalene and the other women after His resurrection all served to elevate the position of women. Roman women had no legal independence or independent property such that unmarried women were not respected in society. Widows had a very low position in society and were required to remarry after the husband's death so as to gain some standing in society. The church's support of widows raised their position. Also Christian values of monogamy, its denial of polygamy, incest, infidelity, divorce, infanticide (girls were more likely to be killed than boys) and abortion positively affected women. Monogamy gave Christian women more equality and security than women of other cultures.

The idea of human rights too finds its cradle and essence in Judeo-Christian ethic. The idea of natural rights can be traced back to Aquinas who believed in a law derived from eternal law. To him actions are judged as good or bad if they confine to reason; thus natural law is a principle woven within human nature. Aquinas continues to influence political and legal philosophers. Common law was clarified with the coming of Christianity to state that *'natural law was not an entity by itself but part of God's created order in nature through which he made all rational human beings aware of what is right and wrong'* (Schmidt 2004). The concept of natural law was expressed by the Apostle Paul when he wrote.

For when Gentiles, who do not have the law, by nature do what the law requires, they are a law to themselves, even though they do not have the law. They show that the work of the law is written on their hearts, while their conscience also bears witness, and their conflicting thought accuse or even excuse them. Romans 2:14-15

Locke states that governments exist to uphold the natural rights of citizens and thus lose legitimacy when they fail to do so. The American Declaration of Independence states that *'whenever any form of government becomes destructive of these ends, it is the right of the people to alter it or abolish it and to institute a new government'*, therefore reinforcing the idea of natural rights deriving from nature. Natural rights are closely related to the term 'self-evident' which also has Christian origins. Gary Amos states, *'To the medievalists, self-evident knowledge was truth known intuitively, as direct revelation from God, without the need for proofs. The term presumed that man was created in the image of God and presumed certain beliefs about man's rationality which can be traced as far back as Augustine in the early 5th Century.'* The preamble of the Magna Carta reflects its strong Christian ties as it starts with, *'John by the grace of God...'* It also states that the charter was made of *'reverence for God and for the salvation of our soul and those of all our ancestors and heirs...'* The Magna Carta was one of the very first documents to lay out the civic liberties of citizens and what was expected of leaders and their subjects regarding these rights.

Jurgen Habermas: Time of Transitions

Universalistic egalitarianism, from which sprang the ideals of freedom and a collective life in solidarity, the autonomous conduct of life and emancipation, the individual morality of conscience, human rights and democracy, is the direct legacy of the Judaic ethic of justice and the Christian ethic of love. This legacy, substantially unchanged, has been the object of continual critical appropriation and reinterpretation. To this day, there is no alternative to it. And in light of the current challenges of a post-national constellation, we continue to draw on the substance of this heritage. Everything else is just idle postmodern talk.

The church was responsible for starting the first formal schools in the West. Christianity's long tradition of teaching from Jesus to the apostles inspired these reforms. Small monastic communities offered the only public education at the time. Although the church was not the first to start formal schools, it was the first to offer public education in an egalitarian manner that made no distinction as to class or gender. Christians such as Aquinas believed that reason was in harmony with faith and that reason contributed to the understanding of revelation. Cathedral schools evolved into the earliest universities which were staffed by monks and friars. In fact the West's most influential universities were founded by the church. Universities in Italian towns like Salerno were leading medical schools, Bologna University was one of the most influential early universities in canon and civil law. In America, education was founded on the backbone of the sixteenth century reformation. Universities whose aim was to apply the Bible to all life emerged. Harvard was one of the first universities to be founded in 1636 with a curriculum that emphasized the study of biblical languages such as Greek, Aramic and Hebrew; logic and theology; and public speaking and rhetoric. Harvard's early motto was *Veritas Christo et Ecclesiae (Truth for Christ and the Church)*, today it is simply *Veritas*. During the inception of universities there was no vast difference between secular and theological education. Among the universities built precisely upon Christian values were Princeton, Brown, Rutgers, Yale, Oxford, King's College, William and Mary and Dartmouth. In evangelized lands the first people to operate schools were Christians. In Africa missionaries built schools, monasteries and hospitals. In India the church built 25 000 schools and colleges. The church remains the main largest nongovernmental provider of education. Noah Webster educator and compiler of the 1828 *An American Dictionary of the English Language wrote,* 'Education without the Bible is useless.'

Christian values and beliefs can also be seen as the spirit behind the West's artistic history. The beauty of the gospel can be seen inspiring the greatest writers, artists and musicians in Western history. It is in no way an exaggeration to credit Christianity for the brilliance of Western art, its values, the hope it provides, the moral pillar it is, is the spirit and soul behind the arts. Renaissance artists such as Raphael, Leonardo Da Vinci, Benini, Michelangelo, Botticelli, Titan and Angelico were inspired by their faith and also sponsored by the church. Catholic monks developed the first forms of modern Western musical notation to standardize liturgy throughout the church. This led directly to the birth and growth of classical music. Many forms of music such as the sonata, the oratorio and the symphony have their roots in Christianity. Most musical forms started as hymns, psalms and spiritual songs. Beethoven's Ode to Joy, Mozart's Ave Verum Corpus, Schubert's Ave Maria, Vivaldi's Gloria and Cesar Franck's Panis angelicus were all great compositions inspired by the faith of the composers. Their work and their music remains some of the greatest compositions in Western history. The Baroque style which encompassed art, music and architecture was encouraged by the post Reformation Catholic Church as a way of religious expression to stimulate religious fervour. Christianity was a great influence to Western worldview; inspiring some of the greatest literature. Suman Theologica by Aquinas is considered one of the most influential works of Western literature. St Augustine of Hippo's Confessions is considered as the first autobiography in Western literature, his writings influenced medieval thought. The bible has contributed greatly to language and literature as well as common thought. From the Scriptures come many words we use today such as *adoption, scapegoat, liberty, ambitious, cucumber* to name a few. Some familiar phrases deriving from the King James Bible translated by William Tyndale include *let there be light, the powers that be, a law unto themselves and fight the good fight.* Alistair McGrath notes, *'Without the King James Bible, there would be no Paradise Lost, no Pilgrim's Progress, no Handel's Messiah, no Negroe spirituals and no Gettysburg Address'.* Biblical themes and words have found their way into the most influential works of literature we still enjoy today such as the works of William Shakespeare, T.S Eliot, William Faulkner, William Blake, Chaucer, Hawthorne, Dante among many others.

Much as contemporary thought has greatly distorted history, Christians were among the first and most influential scientists. To them science was a way to uncover the laws of nature as laid out by God upon creation. *"It was Robert Grosseteste (ca. 1168-1214), a Franciscan bishop and first chancellor of Oxford University, who first proposed the inductive, experimental method and his student, Roger Bacon (1214-94) who asserted that 'all things must be verified by experience.' Nearly three hundred years later Francis Bacon (1561-1626) gave momentum to the inductive method by recording his experimental results. Bacon has been called 'the practical creator of scientific induction.' Besides his scientific interests he also devoted time to theology and wrote treaties on the Psalms and prayer"* (Schmidt 2004). Although I do very little justice on the topic, the historian Lynn White's words that, *'From the thirteenth century onwards into the eighteenth every major scientist, in effect, explained his motivations in religious terms'*, articulate the point I wish to put across. Great scientists in history motivated by their faith were William Occam (1280-1349) who developed the principle of parsimony, Leonardo Da Vinci (1452-1519), Andreas Vesalius (1514-64), Gregor Johann Mendel (1822-1884) who worked in genetics, Galileo, Brahe, Kepler and Copernicus in the field of astronomy, in physics we find Isaac Newton (1642-1727), Leibniz (1646-1716), Pascal (1623-62), Volta (1745-1827), Georg Simon Ohm (1787-1854), Ampere (1775-1836, Faraday (1791-1867) and William Thompson Kelvin (1824-1907). The fathers of modern science saw no discord between faith and science, they believed in a rational God and that rational God who made the world based on natural laws; they saw their duty as scientists was to discover these laws. Without their beliefs science would not be what it is today.

A single chapter of course cannot exhaust the vast, significant and formative place that Christianity holds in the history of mankind. Christians built the first hospitals; their ideals are reflected in the welfare systems and policies of many governments. Their ideals were the matrix of civilization as we know it, their values taught the Western man of the world and how to live in it, why to live in it and to what end, its vision of the world guided their path and its ideals planted the desire for justice in their heartland, its movement and the power of its hope and perfection shaped their soul and directed their aesthetic pursuits. Christianity is alive in the cradle of civilization and in the era of the Western man's awakening it was the calling voice and it was the dawn. In this era of postmodernism, we witness a lot of chaos and in that chaos there is a desperate attempt to carry forth the ideals planted by Christianity in the building of a better world whilst removing God from the equation. It is a pity then that those who champion the so called *good without God* little understand the womb from which that goodness came from and that any attempt to carry forth the good without God will and has led to the total miscarriage of any possibility of meaningful and lasting hope and goodness. Every significant good in the world as we know it was woven from the rich and bounty threads of Christian ethics and if the overwhelming evidence in this discourse cannot convince one of the imprudence of privatizing Christianity; very little else can.

CHRISTIANITY, SOCIETY AND HUMAN NATURE

B

y now I have proven that not only does Christianity not exist in a social vacuum, it aims to alter the social reality around it. Stemming from Jewish history, Christianity stands as the answer to the moral problems colouring the Old Testament and humanity at large. These moral problems find their origin in the Garden of Eden; there we find a different kind of human in Adam and Eve; free from sin and perversion. At the same time it is in Eden that we witness the birth of that sinful and defiled human, the fallen human. As society formed, we find its general corruption coloured in human nature- other schools of thought will deny the rigidity and determinism implied by the existence of such a thing as human nature, however the smallest observation of human history supports such a thing. Thus human nature being the foundation of the nature of the collective life we find through history many periods of moral disquiet and ambivalence. It is God's plight throughout the Old Testament to speak to this human coloured by nature, to draw him or her from the path of corruption to the upright path. The nature of the Jewish law which introduces us to the Jewish lexicon words such as sanctity, purity and unclean shows that what needed cleansing was the human spirit, what needed to be purged was human nature. Thus Jewish religion whilst speaking to the human: it was also condemning the overall and individual human nature, not that there was ever hope that any ethical and moral reasoning or any legal statutes and appeal to the human goodness would alter the actions of the people. It is given to us for us to understand that the purpose of Jewish law was in fact to reveal this human nature and to show the people bound to it by their inability to escape from it, and their inability to be pure.

Christ came at a time of great political unrest and also social and religious strain. Christianity when it emerged, fulfilled the intents of the Jewish law; it transferred those familiar yet foreign words into the hearts of mankind. Jesus the Messiah became once and for all the fulfilment of the promise, the finisher of the moral dilemma that had troubled humanity from the start of time; He became the new nature alive in the humans once bound to sin. And in those moments in human history, those pivotal moments, the moments upon which all other events and time stand looking on tenterhooks, in those moments we witness the birth of a new human and with that human; the hope in a new collective conscience, a new society, a new world. Christianity's mandate for social transformation is self-evident because its principles speak directly of a new human nature opposite to the sinful nature, the same sinful nature that was the bane of God's relationship with man in the old covenant. The transformed human is in a new partnership with God, this human stands with Him in a heavenly divine place of worship, the temple that is in the heart, the heart that is now the dwelling place of God. This new human is called back to God, he stands beside Christ in eternal unity and this new human is able to fulfil the desires of God, they are now the law of his heart. It is a new world in the making.

Christianity offers then the answer against tyranny, against the laws of the world and the base standards of our fallen world; in essence Christianity and its values offer a standard of the perfect society, it offers a straight line to measure against the crooked lines of human nature, it offers a light to ward off the darkness and it is in the lowest moments of mankind that we have witnessed this light shine like a lighthouse, the foundation of our hope.

Christians have indeed changed the world in dramatic and significant ways from ending slavery to championing the rights of the oppressed. Whilst it is true that it has been distorted to justify oppression and domination of others, where it broke out in its true and unadulterated form it was a beacon of hope, a light in the darkness and a gigantic force for change. The rebirth of the being has always been the concern of God; His mission has been and still is to leave nothing as it is by grace. Transformation from the state of ruin to a state of refined glory is God's desire for His people. When He created the world, He presaged this glorious transformation by His Words, *'Let there be Light'*, and the light tore through the darkness and the world was born. For the world God intends to build among His people must follow the same instruction, *'let there be light.'* We have seen in history this light tearing past the darkness and from that, new and better societies emerging.

The abolition of slavery stands today as the greatest moral achievement; the impact it made in social transformation has no parallel. It is arguably the greatest political achievement of what is now known as faith based activism. The abolition movement was carried at the back of the church, its values inspired it and its convictions and dedication to the call of God saw it to the very end. In a time where the collective conscience of the people did not convict them of the cruelty of the slave trade and slavery, Christianity tore through the barriers and shined a light upon the hearts and minds of people, highlighting the immorality of not only slavery but racism. In 1787, the Committee for the abolition of the Slave Trade was established by a group of Quakers and Anglicans in England and by 1833 Parliament had abolished slavery in the British colonies, by 1838 slaves were emancipated and by the 1880s slavery had mostly been extinguished throughout the world. This in itself is a tremendous achievement.

From the establishment of the Committee for the abolition of the Slave Trade, abolitionism rapidly became a mass movement, drawing support from the vast majority of the Christian community. Beginning with the American Quakers who believed that Christianity in its true form should be countercultural and who themselves renounced slaveholding; Christian activists started and organized the abolition movement. Granville Sharp, an Anglican evangelical, advocated for oppressed black Britons in courts from the 1760s. Christian activists worked tirelessly to provide evidence for the horrors of this human traffic, the most notorious of which was the case of the slave ship Zong whose captain had 130 slaves thrown off his ship in order to claim insurance for their deaths. With these horrors coming to light, hundreds of thousands of Britons boycotted goods from slave plantations such as sugar and rum. There occurred a dramatic change in Christian attitudes towards slavery in a single generation and that moral reformation led to great social transformation.

Christian ideals were the heart and fire behind the abolition movement. The Christian abolitionists believed in the universal brotherhood of all people as we have all one Father; God. The conviction that all people were made in the Imago Dei; the image of God and are all precious in His sight strengthened their cause. Their beliefs were opposed to polygenesis which was held by many supporters of racism, instead they took their values from scripture with the belief that all humans are equal because we are all of one origin. Anglican Evangelical Hannah More wrote, *'Respect his image which they bear...they still are men and men shou'd be free'.* Christian benevolence played a pivotal role in the movement. Slave holding was regarded as incompatible with the mercy and benevolence of God. Granville Sharp wrote, *'The glorious system of the gospel destroys all narrow, national partiality and makes us citizens of the world, by obliging us to profess universal benevolence...we are bound as Christians, to commiserate and assist to the utmost of our power all persons in distress and captivity.'*

True to their religious values, the Christian abolitionists adhered to the Golden rule, they imagined themselves in the position of the slaves and their horrification at the idea pushed them to act for change. Liberty was at the heart of the movement, drawing from the Exodus of Israel from Egypt, the abolitionists believed that this was a divine denouncement of the institution of slavery and the oppression of others. Slavery was regarded as opposed with the Declaration of Independence which stated, *'all men are created equal and endowed by their Creator with certain inalienable rights.'* Slavery was regarded as a violation of the natural law and it violated natural rights. Liberty was regarded as a right that could not be given or taken away.

The ending of slavery is regarded as one of the greatest achievements of faith based activism yet, it is by far not the only terrain that the gospel has travelled with its world changing power. Its influence on the civil rights movement was pivotal to the ideals of the movement such as equality for all and non-violent movements. The prominence of Martin Lurther King Jr and other ministers of the struggle is a testament that the movement was religious at heart. Freedom, liberty, respect for all people and the belief in inalienable natural rights grounded in God are central to the Christian religion and these ideals are the heart and cornerstone of international human rights. In the darkest moments of human history Christianity has been a guide and champion for the oppressed a testament of the purpose and power of faith in the world.

POWER IN THE KINGDOM OF GOD

P

OWER- this one word carries with it a great weight, within it lies histories of mankind, the politics of governments, the influence of noblemen and noblewomen, the persuasions of priests, the authority of parents, Empires past and present, hopes of future things. Whatever we may think of it; power is largely viewed as a negative thing, a thing that destroys and does not build, a thing that subjugates relentlessly. History testifies what power is-it defines what is right and what is wrong, what is beautiful and what is not, what is allowed to breathe and what should die. Michel Foucault's revolutionary work on power allowed people to reimagine it not merely as a negative thing but as a potentially positive aspect that is exercised by people through everyday acts. To Foucault, power is everywhere. God Himself is described as ALL POWERFUL, He holds all power, the power to create, destroy, the power to set up kingdoms and lay out their ends, the power over life and death, the power over time and eternity, the power over the destinies of all creatures in the universe; the power to save. Power is complex, certain yet fluid, sought after and yielded by the greatest kings, in the hands of the little infants, it is strength, it is faith, it is hope, it is fought over by many. It is the breath in our lungs and it is the tornado, power is many things all at once and it is one thing altogether. But what is power in the kingdom of God?

Because this essay explores the place of the church in public policy, we will have to look at the power of God in the public space, how is that power exercised and how does it manifest for positive change? Here we will need to walk back through history. We have witnessed the influence that the early church had on the societies it touched and we have seen how the church shaped the modern world. Influence and the ability to change-that is POWER. Yet power as we are used to in the world politics is an overt business of bayonets and soldiers, of strength of arms and propaganda.

Humans are communicative and interactive creatures and it is through our symbolic actions that our beliefs and ideas are expressed and passed on. At the same time humans are political and social creatures; who exists in groups and institutions. In the Christian discourse, we often create a divide between the political and social world and the micro world of everyday interaction. That is to say when we speak of religion and its place in our everyday world we often relegate it a space in our micro sphere .i.e. the sphere of everyday interaction with our friends, family etc. We do this feeling that this is how we safeguard our religion from the world and its institutions. Yet there is no division between the religious, social, economic and political world.

Every action that we make has cultural, social, economic and political consequences; all our actions are political and social statements and also statements of our beliefs. It is in our everyday actions that we propel the world to a better place. As we exist in a social movement world in which activism is on the rise. We all know the world we live in is not perfect, yet revolution and violence are looked towards as the road to a better world. Violence however begets violence and only peace can bring about peace. This peace we profess as the gift of the Prince of Peace is brought about through the conscious actions of every Christian to refuse violence and to embrace pacifism. Wars and other forms of violence are made possible by the willingness of ordinary men and women who profess the faith yet are also willing to go to war. The only way to end war is for us to choose love and hate violence. *'All that a pacifist can undertake-but it is a very great deal-is to refuse to kill, injure, or otherwise cause suffering to another human creature, and untiringly to order his life by the rule of love though others may be captured by hate'* -Vera Brittain. This life choice is the political act of nonviolence the world peace treaty that takes away wars, for the laws we search for, the laws of God that can make the world a better place, these laws exists in our hearts and they can be written upon the face of the world without waiting for the state or the government to make the change, our individual and collective actions towards peace can reshape and refashion the world towards the image of its Creator.

Today we are facing great humanitarian crises, from famine, poverty existent in the world at large, wars and natural disasters. There are enough resources in the world for everyone to live well yet capitalism at both the global, regional and local levels perpetrates social inequality and poverty. Our religious call towards giving and charity is an economic call; our everyday choices whether to give or withhold, to accumulate and consume or otherwise have grand economic consequences. It is through them that we assert or denounce the excesses of capitalism; it is through our daily choices to give that we rewrite economic laws.

Our individual actions contribute to the power dialogue of the world around us. Our discourse, our actions, interactions and the symbols we use to explain our world are all statements we contribute to the power plays in the world around us. It is through this symbolic interaction that worldviews leave their imprints upon the world. Christianity has instructions that tell us how we should interact with each other in all spheres of life either as leaders, with the poor, the oppressed and all these symbolic actions contribute to the painting we place upon the world. Political realities are imprinted upon the world through our everyday actions as well. For example, in class we vote for class monitors as opposed to having a student elect oneself; this symbolic action is an assertion of democracy and people who sit down to watch a royal wedding assert their admiration of the monarchic institution. Christianity too has the law of the Servant Leader; yet do our everyday acts assert this leadership model or regardless of our beliefs do we assert in our symbolic actions other political models? A Christian leader whether political or religious or otherwise must through everyday actions of interaction, serving, accumulating, controlling and deciding to assert humility, service and pacifism. It is through these actions that the world can change, the moral choices that reflect the basis of our beliefs; the very beliefs that are the laws of God's kingdom.

We are through our discursive acts cultural ambassadors of our beliefs; beliefs that should not be relegated to the sphere of rituals and religion alone because the religion is the life and the life is lived within many terrains that reflect who we are. This form of power is perhaps more powerful than the ammunitions that assert wars or the grand structures, we see all around us. Power in the world is overt power, exercised through statutes and laws, through arms and mass media. Power in the kingdom of God is innate, it lives with the spirit of the redeemed, a kingdom within. Power as a concept is associated with influence, authority, control and dominance. In the world this is exercised through external structures, a power that is exerted from the outside, almost always forcefully encroaching upon the liberty of the mass. We rely on legal statutes, the police to demarcate our behaviours and ensure through threats of punishments that social order is maintained. States are backed by the legitimate use of force to ensure that society complies with its demands.

Yet Foucault reminds us that *'power is everywhere'*, diffused and embodied in discourse, knowledge and *'regimes of truth'* (Foucault 1991). He challenges the idea that power is wielded by people or groups by way of sovereign acts of domination or coercion. He sees it as dispersed and pervasive, not concentrated and discursive. The agency of actors is central to Foucault's conception of power. And this non-coercive conception of power existing at the micro level is akin to power in the kingdom of God. The laws of God exist in the hearts of people, their authority and influence enforced by the Holy Spirit who inspires acts of love and kindness. The obedience to the kingdom laws is not dependent upon external force but by the internal force of the Holy Spirit through the power of the blood. Those who receive salvation are redeemed and made into a new creation. This new creation made like Christ is given the righteousness of God. It is at the micro level; of the person doing acts of goodness everyday- the person who denies violence, who gives to the poor, who loves their neighbour as self, who serves as a leader; that power is exercised.

For Foucault power is not necessarily a negative thing; it is also productive and positive. *'We must cease once and for all to describe the effects of power in negative terms: it 'excludes' it 'represses', it 'censors', it 'abstracts', it 'masks', it 'conceals'. In fact power produces; it produces reality; it produces domains of objects and rituals of truth.'* (Foucault 1991). We have seen in the church the productive power of the church where the world aimed to destroy. Power in the church first destroys the negative, base and destructive influences within man and replaces these with the seeds of love and kindness, seeds that when planted in the world the church operated in ended slavery, produced communities based on egalitarianism and communal ownership, raised the position of women and children, built schools and hospitals, sought after knowledge, produced great art, music and literature. The essence, culture and beauty of the church is power at work. The same creative power that at the beginning of time spoke creation into being. It was power that brought everything into being, power by which that creation endures and multiplies and it is that same power of the Word that allowed and still allows the good works of the church.

Whilst the state largely relies on overt and punitive measures to repress deviant and destructive behaviour in society, whether their standards are just or otherwise; in the kingdom of God there is self-surveillance. Foucault sees power as an everyday, socialized and embodied phenomenon. Norms and values become a central aspect in individual lives that there is really no need for severe measures of discipline. People regulate their own behaviours through the internalization of the values, norms and teachings of the church and the example of Christ. This form of power is practiced every day; in every aspect of life challenging contradictory ideals and institutions as well as enforcing the ideals of the church. This is perhaps the highest form of power, displayed in language and discourse, actions and symbols and symbolic action; small actions compared to the gigantic power structures we see in the institutions about us but with titanic power for authentic change. Arundhati Roy puts it this way, *'colourful demonstrations and weekend marches are vital but alone are not powerful enough to stop wars. Wars will be stopped only when soldiers refuse to fight, when workers refuse to load weapons onto ships and aircraft, when people boycott the economic outposts of Empire that are strung across the globe'.*

CONCLUSION

The City of God

T

ogether we have travelled the passages of history and have seen the grand and magnificent, world altering power of the church. We have witnessed it foreshadowed in the works of the ancient prophets and the law, we have watched it in its cradle as the hope for eternal peace and we testify that the vast good that exists in the world today rests upon its back, carried by it even as the world attempts to untether it and erase it from history. Humanism with its call for separation of the Church and the state has launched a war upon the church, a war that has progressively driven it to the margins of society and public policy. The postmodern church has done little to rectify this as it takes what it wants from the gospel and leaves what it does not desire. With alarming certainty, the church is losing social significance and for as long as it does nothing noteworthy for the wellbeing of humanity, it is in danger of becoming inconsequential.

There are a myriad of divergent voices from varying spaces, each of them vehement for their causes. It is not an understatement to state that the contemporary society is perhaps the most socially conscious in history, but it is also a postmodern society, denial of individual subjectivity is almost as criminal as direct violation of social laws. It is a pluralistic society in which every voice deserves an audience, yet because these ideals were penned in direct opposition to what was viewed as the *moral dictatorship of the church'*, the church's voice is often viewed as not having a legitimate space in public policy. Its values are largely seen as the dissident voices causing disharmony to the postmodern, free thinking choir of reason. It is true that the church has to come to grips with the fact that the society it now finds itself in is a system based in part of the ideals adopted from the church yet with almost draconian opposition to God. But history shows us that the church was not planted in soils ready to receive it yet in the desert of opposition, grew the garden of God and from it came bountiful fruits of the spirit because the church remained what it was, that which belongs to God- primarily and exclusively.

The church which Jesus referred to as the light of the world has always stood as the dichotomous opposite of the world. Woven into the fabric of the world through centuries of God's work among men; it has always been understood as the final and ultimate will of God for His creation. It is the design crocheted by the hands of God, with intricate patterns of scarlet thread, its message is one of hope and salvation through Jesus Christ, Him who is the first and last. The first because He is the Word by which everything was created and the Last because it is to Him that all must return. And creation is intended to return to Him as mirrors of Him. The argument for Christian involvement in public space is incomplete without an understanding of the relevance of Christianity for us today. Those who oppose Christian involvement in public policy believe that the cosmic morality of Christianity is outdated and that humans have free will and reason enough to forge their own moral compass. I believe the previous segments have already established that Christianity is not the antonym of reason and that far from being outdated its ideals are the cradle in which the modern world was nursed. The contemporary society prides itself in being a pluralistic society, if so then all voices without exclusion must be granted an audience, the church included. If indeed we are a free inquiry society, then the conclusions and reasons of the church should not be seen as a threat to a society willing and keen to be diverse.

The church of Christ is exclusive. When Jesus came unto the world, His kingdom was understood as the kingdom of heaven, different from the world of men. Yet God descended upon the world He created to plant the seeds of His kingdom, to lay the foundation of His House, to make the church His temple and the redeemed His vessels. It is upon this earthly fallen kingdom that He intends to plant His feet and it is upon this earthly fallen world that He laid the design of His new creation of which He is the first born. It is a future perfect world that we witness in the church, a perfection that will be completed in heaven but His hands are sculpturing it; refining the sharp edges and polishing the ragged surfaces until we are His heritage, His bride, His children restored to Him.

The church remains relevant today because we are in the making, moving forward to a time to come, of which the scriptures say, *'every knee shall bow and every tongue shall confess His name'*. Christianity like every other worldview has beliefs about reality, about the ultimate purpose of humanity and about our relationship with our creator; our nature and His nature. The gospel is the good news of the redeemed and the redeemed are tasked to be the light of the world. Christianity does not exist in a social vacuum and the communal beliefs of the church are meant to be lived in public life. Compartmentalization of the private and public space in matters of faith is impractical and impossible because our private convictions direct our public actions. These communal ideals have to do with the church's stance towards violence and war, social justice, leadership, service, human rights and even economics.

Jesus came as the light of the world and His teachings were not mere theory; but they were meant to be followed and lived out. We often assume that as we speak of the religious, it is confined to rituals alone; however every action whether economic, social, political or cultural is a spiritual statement. Perhaps the greatest ideology of our time is the assumption that compartmentalization of different aspects of human life is possible and even practical. Jesus' teachings had a historical, social and political bearing and through and through those teachings were religious; it is the spiritual life that was meant to be the directive of the cultural, social, political and economic. The church as the ecclesia is not a body of people sharing similar beliefs who only meet on designated days for worship and sermons, no, the church is a body of people meant to represent Christ in the world. We are to be His hands and feet taking directive from what He the head has to say. Jesus responded to the judicial, religious, social, political, economic and intellectual issues of the society around Him and the world at large. The *'love your neighbour as yourself'* is given not as an ideal beautiful to think of but as a command that has the capacity to change the world. All systems of ideas respond to the environment that humans find themselves in contrary to what we often think that we are only to look forward to the world to come, but the world to come must be reflected by our actions here in the world of the living. As Christians we are called to be the advocates and defenders, the people of justice, the moral compasses of the world, the defenders of peace and deniers of war; Christianity was never meant to be a passive belief yet even in our silence and inactivity, we arm and strengthen the powers of chaos and thus say something. We are through our moral, social, cultural and theoretical choices meant to be the bearers of the universality of God's truth in an elaborate and practical way, for it is in action that the beauty of our beliefs is witnessed to the world. We stand at the backdrop of a world with an intellectual history of denying God, yet it is only through our actions and not merely our words that our truth is made evident, thus the call to action. We stand at the backdrop of a world ridden by wars, ironically it is the so called Christian nations that most times start these wars, and Christians that enlist as soldiers directed by the belief that there is honour in war and that it is a necessary part of human life. We live in a world with suffering millions and yet it is the church that supports materialism and consumerism when we are supposed to be the defenders of the poor and downtrodden, we are supposed to be the opposers of arrogant wealth and promoters of not only philanthropy but equality in everything. The world might be in darkness but the church which was called the light of the world, the salt of the world is doing little to let the light shine to the world. No amount of protest or revolution can make the world a better place, only the inner revolution is the hope, and not the artificial change we find through education but the change that comes through salvation is the hope. The church has a duty to God and God's call for His people is that they be a service to others indiscriminate of what their beliefs are. The Christian values of justice, hope, grace, love, non-violence, service, charity and peace have all the capacity to change the world if rightly acted upon.

ABOUT THE AUTHOR

Chiedza Nyanyiwa is an essayist and novelist born in Harare, Zimbabwe. She is a child rights practitioner by profession and founder of Children's Republic Association, an NGO that advocates for the rights of marginalized children. She holds a bachelor's degree in Sociology and Gender development and a Master of Child Sensitive Social Policies degree from Women's University in Africa. When she is not writing or working, Chiedza spends her time reading or developing her passion for art. The Covenant of Life and Other Essays is her debut book.

REFERENCES

Arnold, E. (1997). *The Early Christians in their own words.* The Plough Publishing House.

Brittain, V. (2014). *Testament of Youth.* Vigaro Press.

Christian Education. (n.d.). Retrieved from Willian Bradford Christian School: www.wbcslions.org

F Engels and K Marx. (2015). *The Communist Manifesto.* Penguin Classics.

Foucault, M. (1991). *Discipline and punish; the birth of the prison.* New York: Random House.

Foucault, M. (1994). *The subject and power;in Foubi; Power, Essential works of Foucault.* London: Penguin Books.

Fowler, J. A. (2011). *Man as God intended.* Cly Publishing.

Gushee, D. P. (2014). *In the Fray; Contesting Christian Public Ethics.* Oregon: Cscade Books.

Habermas, J. (2006). *Time of Translations.* Polity.

Jean Paul Ritcher- The Life of Christ. (n.d.). Retrieved from Lifeoverbeach: www.lifeoverbeach.wordpress.com

John Witte Jr and Justin J Latterell. (n.d.). Christianity and Human Rights; Past Contributions and future Challenges. *Journal of*

Law and Religion. Retrieved from Cambridge University Press: www.jstor.org

Jr, L. W. (1967). The historical roots of our Ecological crisis. *Science 155:1203-1207*.

Marmor, A. (2011). *Philosophy of Law*. Princeton University Press.

McGrath, A. (2008). *In the beginning; the story of the King Jmes Bible and how it changed a nation, a language and a culture*. Knopf Douleday Publishing Group.

Northurp, S. (2014). *Twelve Years a Slave*. William Collins.

Packer, J. I. (n.d.). The plan of God. www.the-highway.com.

Rene Cassin-Biographical. (n.d.). Retrieved from Nobel Prize Outreach: www.nobelprize.org

Rorty, R. (1994). *Religion as a Conversation Stopper in Philosophy and Social hope*. New York: Penguin.

Roy, A. (2004). *Public Power in the Age of Empire*. Seven Stories Press.

Sartre, J. P. (2007). *Humanism-Existentialism is a humanism*. Yale University Press.

Schmidt, A. J. (2004). *How Christianity Changed the World*. Zondervan.

Sharp, G. (1775). An Essay on Slavery.

Sweet, W. (1999). *Religious belief, Political Culture and Community*. Bristol: Thoemmes Press.

Tolstoy, L. (1895). *Christianity and Patriotism as translatated in the Novels and other works of Lyof N Tolstoi Vol 20*.

Tolstoy, L. (1990). *Government is violence; Essays on Anarchism and Pacifism*. Phoenix Press.

Tolstoy, L. (2012). *The Kingdom of God is within You translated by Constance Garnett*. Courier Corporations.

Weeks, D. L. (1998). Carl F H Henry's moral arguments for evangelical political activism. *Journal of Church and State Vol 40*.

Wesley, J. (1754). *Explanatory notes upon the New Testament.* New York: Cartor and Porter.

Wilson, H. (2016). Justice from God's perspective; How Christianity theology can transform a broken world. *NACSW Convention.* Cincinnati, OH.

Wilson, t. b. (n.d.). *The Writings of Clement Alexandria.* Retrieved from Gutenberg: www.gutenberg.com